Pride of the Land

An Affectionate History of
Brandon's Agricultural Exhibitions

Pride of the Land

Ken Coates • Fred McGuinness

1985
Peguis Publishers Limited • Winnipeg Canada

Canadian Cataloguing in Publication Data

Coates, Kenneth, 1956-
    Pride of the land

    Includes index.
    ISBN 0-920541-01-1

1. Agricultural exhibitions — Manitoba —
Brandon — History. 2. Provincial Exhibition
of Manitoba (Brandon, Man.) — History. 3.
Royal Manitoba Winter Fair (Brandon, Man.) —
History. 4. Brandon (Man.) — Fairs — History.
I. McGuinness, Fred. II. Title.
S557.C32M34 1985   630'.74'011273
                        C85-091627-5

Copyright ©Kenneth Stephen Coates and

Frederick George McGuinness, 1985

All rights reserved

Book design — Pat Stanton

Cover photography — Paul Martens

Special events coordination, Brandon —

Brandon University Press

Printed and bound in Canada

 è **&** *Table of Contents*

THIS BOOK IS THE DIRECT RESULT of a suggestion made by Mr. Reg Forbes. As a long-time agriculturist, he felt that the story of fairs and exhibitions should be recorded in permanent form. The authors commend him for his initiative and thank him for his support during the writing process.

Brandon University Press was closely associated with the authors in the preparation of the text. Facilities and support materials were provided and special efforts expended on promotion of the book in the Brandon area. Their generosity is hereby acknowledged with sincere thanks.

With the financial assistance of the Provincial Exhibition of Manitoba, Career Start Manitoba and the Manitoba Heritage Foundation, it was possible to employ four student/researchers. It was a distinct pleasure to work with Bruce Stadfeld, who supervised the group, Diane Fowler, Rob McGarva and Byron Williams. The depth of their interest in this assignment is reflected in the number of late nights and weekends which they contributed to this project. Without their spirited assistance this book would not have been possible, or working on it as enjoyable.

Many persons assisted us with facts, pictures and mementos. Noteworthy among them were Mr. George MacArthur, Mr. J.I. Moffatt, Mr. Hope Turner, Mr. David Montgomery, Mr. and Mrs. Laurence Stuckey, Mr. and Mrs. P.A. McPhail, and the Daly House Museum. Eileen McFadden kindly allowed the research team to use the facilities of the Brandon University Archives, where the exhibition records are stored. We extend our thanks as well to Dr. Peter Hordern, Dean of Arts, Dr. W.R. Morrison, Chairman of the Department of History, and the Board of Governors of Brandon University for their help in the preparation of this book.

Special thanks are reserved for Mary Scorer and Mary Dixon, past and present owners of Peguis Publishers Limited, for their enthusiasm and interest in the history of Brandon's fairs. Chapter three is for Lexi Morling, who knows why.

A final acknowledgement is reserved for our wives, Cathy Coates and Christine McGuinness, who listened to numerous tales of our discoveries. This book is dedicated to them, in hopes that it will compensate for our lengthy and frequent absences.

Ken Coates and Fred McGuinness, Brandon, 1985

Chapter One

1882 - 1912

Years of Hope

1   *The oldest picture of Brandon known to exist, c.1882. It shows the north side of Rosser Avenue between 9th and 10th Streets.*

2   *Charles Whitehead, pioneer Brandon merchant who organized and served as president of the first fair. His farm two miles south of Brandon on present-day Highway #10 was "contract #1," the first parcel of property ever sold by Canadian Pacific.*

THE REGION BRISTLED with anticipation and energy. After years of delay, the Canadian Pacific Railway was completing plans to push the mainline west from Winnipeg toward the Rocky Mountains. For those few pioneers who had ventured forth into the unorganized territories west of Portage La Prairie, the event was highly significant. They knew of the agricultural potential of the land west of the boundary of the tiny province of Manitoba; they knew too that their dreams and ambitions would remain unrealized without the iron road. Now, finally, the word had come: the railway was on its way.

For those settlers who had homesteaded in such places as Grand Valley and the Brandon Hills, the main question was the location of the first divisional townsite. Speculators, many of whom had earlier gambled on Rapid City, now placed their money on Grand Valley, a small town on the banks of the Assiniboine River. General Thomas L. Rosser, chief engineer for the prairie section of the Canadian Pacific Railway's mainline, balked at the price demanded by John McVicar, owner of the Grand Valley townsite, and shared the concerns of many that the location was susceptible to flooding. Early in May 1881, Rosser decided on a new location, two miles west of Grand Valley. By the end of the month, city lots were on sale and the first load of lumber had arrived. Within a year, on 20 May 1882, the settlement had been formally incorporated as the City of Brandon.

Like so many prairie towns established in the late nineteenth century, Brandon existed on hope, potential and the energy of its founding citizens. Its future depended on the economic growth of the surrounding territory. In all areas, Brandon soon proved to be particularly well blessed. Men like Charles Whitehead, lumberman and real estate agent, W.J. White, publisher of the *Brandon Sun*, Thomas Mayne Daly, Brandon's first lawyer and first mayor, Clifford and Arthur Sifton, both to become famous western Canadian politicians, and Pat Burns, later one of Canada's richest cattle barons, were drawn by the prospects of the first "Instant City" on the Canadian plains. They were not to be disappointed, for Brandon soon proved to be more than just a rail centre.

The city flourished in large measure because of the strength and diversity of the farming community which followed the railway west. Settlers arriving to try their hand at prairie agriculture used Brandon as a jumping-off point; and in a few years cattlemen, horse breeders and wheat farmers began to occupy the fertile lands in the surrounding area. The city fathers recognized at a very early date the vital relationship between the town and the farm. Brandon was an agricultural service centre, its prosperity dependent upon the success of the farmers and livestock men. Nothing would demonstrate this close relationship more clearly than the agricultural exhibition.

The first Brandon fair was held only five months after incorporation. The city was not alone in recognizing the value of an agricultural exhibition. Fairs had a rich heritage, both in the Old World and in North America. For generations, they had provided an opportunity for people to gather together for business, friendly competition and entertainment. In the 18th century, British aristocrats had instituted major changes in the form and function of the yearly rituals. They were particularly anxious to encourage innovation and greater production, and so sponsored a variety of competitions designed to highlight excellence in agriculture.

The concept spread quickly, crossing the Atlantic Ocean with the British colonists to North America. Using fairs to promote agriculture seemed particularly relevant in the New World, where pioneer farmers struggled to adapt their crops, livestock and farming techniques of the Old World to an unfamiliar environment. The fairs were also useful in promoting the agricultural potential of newly opened regions, demonstrating to local residents, would-be settlers, businessmen and government the great future of the new land.

In 1870, following the Red River Resistance and the entrance

3   *The new horse stable,*
Brandon fair, 1900.

4   *New cattle building, Brandon fair, 1900.*

5   *The first Crystal Palace, built in 1884. This photo shows a later addition c. 1900.*

5

of Manitoba into Confederation, settlers from central Canada began to venture west. They came in small numbers, certainly not in droves as the federal government had hoped, bringing with them the values and traditions of their homelands. The first attempt at an agricultural fair in the west occurred at Fort Garry in 1871. Portage La Prairie soon followed. In 1872, the Marquette Agricultural Society hosted a fall fair in Portage, drawing some 400 entries and establishing the Portage exhibition as the first permanent prairie fair.

The pattern had been set. Any self-respecting town anxious to put its name on the agricultural map had to host a fair. By 1882, seventeen towns held agricultural exhibitions. One of those towns was Brandon.

The community hardly seemed ready for an agricultural fair in the spring of 1882. The town was scarcely a year old, with rutted and muddy streets, and only some 700 residents within its borders. But the bustle, clamor and confusion of this overnight growth pointed to a rosy future. Buildings were going up as fast as lumber could be delivered. Businessmen and professionals arrived daily to add to the list of stores and services available. The town was constantly working on the roads, adding culverts and sidewalks in an effort to give the development a more settled aspect.

Both townfolk and farmers recognized the need for a fair. The Brandonites were anxious to demonstrate the importance of their new city. The farmers hoped that an agricultural exhibition would bring greater attention to the region's potential. In time-honored fashion, they agreed that an agricultural exhibition, scheduled for October 1882, would be an appropriate means of demonstrating the prospects of their town and region, and the Brandon Agricultural Society was formed.

The first board of directors had an obvious agricultural bias. The members' personal and commercial interests were in the farming and cattle-raising communities of western Manitoba.

Several of the directors, including J.W. Vantassel, Charles Pilling and George Halse, were listed in the city directory of 1883 as farmers. J. E. Smith was a real estate broker, farm implement dealer and owner of a livery stable. William Johnson and R.T. Evans were also farm implement dealers. Thomas Lockhart was an agent for the Manitoba and Northwest Loan Company, a firm with substantial financial interests in western Manitoba agriculture. These directors were clearly farm men, deeply concerned with developing the area's agricultural potential.

Few records remain from that first fair. Local businessmen put up some $200 in prize money, and called for entries for cattle, horses, pigs, poultry and grains. Poor weather dampened the expected high spirits of the first fair, and resulted in only a smattering of entries for the competitions. It was a modest beginning for what one historian of western Canadian fairs would later call the "Mother of Exhibitions."

The exhibition promoters were not deterred by the combination of hasty planning and bad weather. Preparations began almost immediately for the next year's fair, again scheduled for October in hopes that the fall dates would allow all farmers and livestock breeders to attend. A generous $2,500 donation from city council and a further grant of $2,000 from the Brandon district council allowed the Brandon Agricultural Society to purchase a small lot south of the city and to erect a "Crystal Palace," immodestly named after the handsome structure erected for the 1851 London International Exposition. A $2,100 grant from the provincial government further aided the Society's efforts.

THE SECOND ANNUAL EXHIBITION proceeded much more favorably than the first. Over 730 entries were received, providing for strong competition in such areas as horses, vegetables, ladies' work and fine arts. The one disappointment, and it was significant, was the cattle competition which drew only 31 entries. Still, the directors were well pleased with this second effort. As President Charles Whitehead noted in his speech to the annual meeting: "If this county does not beat every other in agriculture, stock raising and general farming it will be no fault of the Brandon Agricultural Society."

Despite Whitehead's brave words, the agricultural exhibition was not proceeding as well as hoped. The fall schedule, though standard for agricultural fairs, was often in conflict with harvesting or hampered by poor weather. The *Brandon Sun* plumbed the essence of the problem following another less than successful fair in 1884:

> The slim turnout of the farming community is attributable, in a great degree, to the backwardness of the harvest: there being still a large acreage to be yet stacked. It is a great pity, however, that in such a fine farming country more interest has not been shown by those who are mainly benefited by a good display of farm productions. If the heads of the households had taken half the interest in the show that their "better halves" have, the display of grains would not have been limited to a single bushel of oats. It is rather humiliating to think that with the hundreds of [bushels of] first-class wheat that have been grown in this country, that not a single farmer had pluck enough to show a sample of wheat.

Unfortunately, there were other critics and other complaints, all of which boded poorly for the Brandon fair. Some wondered aloud if the directors had done enough to promote the fair locally, claiming that area farmers had received little information or encouragement to attend. Though the local press and most local residents supported the work and purpose of the exhibition, the modest returns and poor turn-out for the fall show raised serious questions about the fair's future.

The Brandon Agricultural Society certainly caused some of its own problems, but often unforeseen difficulties emerged. The provincial government, which tended to look upon requests for assistance from Brandon with considerable hesitation, created a major financial mess which all but killed the annual show. The government had, in 1885, indicated that a grant of $1,500 to $2,000 would be forthcoming. The association proceeded on that assumption, only to discover to their horror that the actual grant was only $250.

Having already overspent, the directors scrambled to bring their finances back in order. Appeals were made to the province and to city council for greater assistance, though neither government offered much help. The directors were forced to dip into their own pockets to stave off financial disaster, offering personal guarantees to the bank in order to keep the fair solvent.

The immediate crisis was averted, but the financial distress forced the association to consider the future of the fair. The grandiose dreams of the first years had not been realized, though the association had an excellent site and had started construction of a handsome set of buildings. They had the facilities; they just had not attracted the exhibitors or the spectators. To many in town, the problem lay with the timing. The fall was typically a busy time for prairie wheat farmers, and the Brandon fair did not yet have enough to offer to draw the men away from their fields at that key time of the year.

By 1888, after a series of problems with the weather during the October show and another very modest attendance at the fair, the directors voted in favour of shifting the fair to the summer. They knew they were taking something of a gamble, for most rural fairs were held after harvest. As association secretary E. Fitz Bucke noted: "As it is found impossible to make (the) fall exhibition a success, it is intended to hold the annual fair about the first week of August; that being a time when a holiday can be indulged in by the farmers without loss to them."

The decision was taken with some chagrin, for it involved an admission that the first seven years worth of work had been unsuccessful. Though the public generally applauded the move, some further reservations were voiced. Since the fair was obviously

❧ *1889 24 January*

*"There have been 2210
horses sold in Brandon
last summer, the prices netting
very nearly a quarter of a
million of dollars. At an
auction sale on Monday last,
at the Beaubier House, a
farm near Kemnay was sold
for the sum of $1,600 to
Mr. Senkbeil, also of Kemnay."*
from the *Brandon Mail.*

6 *Experimental Farm,
Brandon, 1905. Early super-
intendents maintained a
close relationship with the
summer fairs during the
period of settlement, using
them as a means of displaying the results of their research.*

ɝ❧ 1889 25 April

"On Friday last as the Atlantic Express was nearing the station, the Agricultural Society under the direction of President Vantassel made hurried arrangement, and had all the owners of horses in the city form a procession on Pacific Avenue. There were over 20 horses in the line, Clydes, Shires, Percheron, Norman, Roadster, General Purpose and Blood. They were a credit to the city. A jackass brought up the rear. They were afterwards photographed. Besides the horses exhibited, throughout the district surrounding but not in the city that day, are horses that will compare favorably with the best. Sir Charles Tupper who was passing east at the time was an interested spectator."
from the *Brandon Mail.*

7 *Kennedy's harvest outfit, Brandon district, c.1890.*

in a state of flux, some people suggested that it was time to make the fair more interesting. The editor of the *Brandon Sun* commented,

> For some years the interest in agricultural exhibitions has only been maintained when the management with a view of making a financial success of the exhibition has digressed from the cast iron rules, and introduced features that were evidently more attractive to the general public than a large squash or a thoroughbred sheep.

The *Sun* had touched on a key point, and a sore spot for other western fairs as well. Though their central purpose was to promote agricultural excellence, the reality was that few city people were truly interested in livestock and grain shows.

The dilemma facing the Brandon fair was that it had to satisfy two audiences. The 22 fairs on the western Manitoba rural fall fair circuit knew their audiences. They appealed directly to the farmers, offering agricultural competitions, sporting events and social gatherings. As a regional centre with a growing urban population, Brandon demanded and needed more to make the fair viable. The agricultural competitions were necessary to attract the farmers, but even the farmers wanted the spice and excitement of a well-rounded exhibition. More importantly, the townsfolk of Brandon had demonstrated their apathy towards the agricultural displays. The association would have to do more than just change the dates to make the summer fair a success.

THE FIRST BRANDON SUMMER FAIR was held in July 1889, and exceeded all expectations. The timing clearly suited area farmers, for they attended in large numbers. The number of entries in the livestock competitions was the highest ever, justifying the shift in dates. Local businessmen also awakened to the exciting commercial prospects of the exhibition. Seldom did so many farmers gather in one place at one time. Farm implement dealers lined the fair grounds with threshers, reapers, traction engines and other machinery. Reports of heavy sales and great interest ensured that they would be back with their displays in future years.

The commercial benefits of the exhibition indicated the great potential of this meeting place between farm and city. As one commentator noted before the 1890 exhibition:

> The merchants and tradesmen will make displays of their merchandise, not in competition for prizes, but simply to afford visitors to the Fair an opportunity of knowing what goods can be obtained in this city and at what prices. It is only one way of letting people know the advantages to be had by trading here; or in other words, a highly practical advertisement for the city. No doubt the exhibitors will be repaid for their time and trouble, for we all know the truth of the saying, 'what the eye sees, the heart craves.'

The directors' gamble, taken in an attempt to save their exhibition, had paid off. The public, both urban and rural, enjoyed the summer fair, the number of competitors had increased substantially, and the prospects for the future suddenly looked very bright.

Over the following few years, efforts were made to spice up the proceedings. Baseball and lacrosse tournaments, band competitions, tug-o-war events, childrens' races, school parades, horse races, hurdle races and an ever increasing number of commercial exhibits, including many from national manufacturing companies, added to the variety and excitement of the annual show. Though plans did not always work out well—the offer of a $100 prize to the best band in 1891 failed to attract a single entry—the effort was generally well rewarded. The fair was changing very rapidly from its early days as an agricultural competition and from all reports the people welcomed the alterations.

The Brandon fair did not forget its agricultural origins. As farming and livestock industries expanded through the 1880s and 1890s, it became ever more obvious that the future of Brandon

The exhibition report in the Brandon Mail includes the following, "Though the display in the classes was larger than that of former years, yet in an agricultural district like this it might have been more extensive. The Brandon Hills Dairy Association had a fine lot of factory cheese."

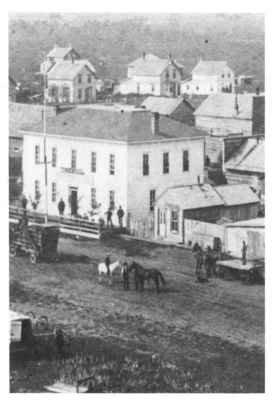

8   *Early Brandon c. 1890.*

and the rural economy were permanently intertwined. The exhibition could not, and to the directors' credit did not, waver in its encouragement of agricultural excellence. As the fair grew, so did its agricultural sections, with impressive prize lists and an increased number of entries.

The farmers' interest in the Brandon fair was enhanced by the presence in town of a Dominion Agricultural Experimental Station. The research centre was at the forefront of agricultural innovation in western Canada, testing new strains of wheat and new methods of cultivation, offering advice to farmers and cattlemen, and generally assisting the improvement of the agricultural economy. The experimental station also maintained a close relationship with the exhibition, for the activities of the two organizations were complementary.

Both the research station and the fair were designed to highlight agricultural excellence and improve farm and cattle-raising standards. The marriage of interests was obvious. S.A. Bedford, first superintendent of the Brandon Experimental Station, was an active member of the exhibition association and ensured that the station placed a prominent display in the yearly fair. It provided the station with an excellent opportunity to educate area farmers on the most recent improvements in prairie agriculture.

The coincidence of interests went one step further. The mere presence in Brandon of the experimental station gave further weight to the city's claim as one of the West's premier agricultural centres. Brandon, the city's promoters loudly proclaimed, had advantages which outstripped other comparable cities. Farmers coming for the exhibition competitions would have the opportunity to visit the experimental station, making the city a mecca for those interested in agricultural progress.

The claim carried all the boastful excess of the urban booster, but it pointed to a central concern for the city and surrounding area. Brandonites were all too aware of the metropolitan aspirations of Winnipeg, and very much concerned about the larger city's often imperialistic designs on the province. Appropriately, the exhibition became a major focus for what was developing into a very vibrant inter-city rivalry.

WINNIPEG, LIKE PORTAGE LA PRAIRIE, BRANDON and other centres, understood the importance of establishing an exhibition as part of the overall promotion of the city. An attempt to start an agricultural show in 1871 had failed, although exhibition supporters in the city and across the river in St. Boniface organized several successful Provincial Exhibitions. Citizens in western Manitoba recoiled at the impertinence of the capital city. Brandon was the agricultural centre of Manitoba, and Winnipeg's attempt to host a farmers' fair smacked of pure folly and opportunism.

The battle had been joined as early as 1883. Following the first Brandon exhibition, President Charles Whitehead and Secretary Thomas Lockhart petitioned the Manitoba Board of Agriculture to designate Brandon's fair as the Provincial Exhibition for 1884. It almost worked. Only some behind-the-scenes negotiating by representatives from Portage La Prairie and Winnipeg prevented Brandon from getting the highly desired designation. The exhibition promoters from Brandon would not soon give up.

On the heels of the 1885 Provincial Exhibition, hosted again in Winnipeg, the editor of the *Brandon Sun* caustically commented:

> The provincial exhibition is over, and a greater failure has not been known in the province. Winnipeg has been boomed all that it can be, and the sooner the town wiseacres there learn that it is impossible to make brick without straw, or make a successful agricultural exhibition where the exhibits have to be carried hundreds of miles, the sooner will a provincial exhibition prove a success.

The attacks continued over the years, reflecting Brandon's desire for urban prominence, a certain jealousy over the number

1897 8 April

"It appears that everything was not smooth sailing at the meeting of the Agricultural and Arts Association on Friday last, a difference arising with a few over the election of Mr. D.M. McMillan as secretary-treasurer. When it was decided that a majority of ballots cast should decide the selection, that should end it. If another method was considered preferable it should have been advanced before the choice was made. Mr. McMillan is no more like the Pope, infallible, than others of the human family, but he is one of the oldest residents of the place, and it yet remains for the man to raise the first objections to his business record. He was secretary-treasurer of the city during the most complicated portion of its financial history, and every one of his methods was found to be correct, without a dollar of an irregularity in any way, shape or form. It is true that in some of his ways he is a little brusque, but beneath that brusque exterior lies the very best of good nature and agreeableness."
from the *Brandon Mail.*

of provincial facilities and grants given to the capital city, and the more logical argument that Winnipeg was an imperfect selection for the site of the province's principle agricultural exhibition.

To the city's promoters at least, Brandon was a far more appropriate site for the annual celebration of Manitoba's agricultural success. It seemed only logical that the western Manitoba city, more centrally-located for farmers and cattlemen, should host the province's largest exhibition and only proper that the "Provincial" designation and attending grants should follow. Breaking Winnipeg's hold on such privileges proved rather difficult.

For the time, Brandon's exhibition association could do little to alter the situation. Western Manitobans seemed to take some delight in the continuing difficulties with the Winnipeg fair, though their pleasure at the city's distress was offset by the repeated provincial grants allocated to Winnipeg. The exhibition controversy was but one part of the battle between Winnipeg and the rest of the province. As one commentator noted, "Some of them (Winnipeg politicians) do not appear to have learned yet that Winnipeg does not comprise and control the whole of Manitoba." To the politicians, businessmen and citizens of Brandon, it seemed obvious that the location of their city outshone that of their rival on the banks of the Red. As the agricultural prospects of the province improved and after the trickle of immigrants to the west turned into a veritable flood during the late 1890s, it seemed likely that Brandon's geographic and economic advantages would soon push the city to the forefront. In the fashion of nineteenth century urban boosters, the town's promoters dreamt big dreams and forecast a bright future for their city.

The exhibition was to be the beacon of Brandon's prosperity, a signpost of what the city and area had achieved, a mark of what the future held. If Brandon was to be a great city, if it was to attract industry and convince investors of its potential, it became increasingly important that the exhibition diversify from its singular agricultural base. The annual fair was the chance to put Brandon

and Western Manitoba on display; it was vital that all the commercial and economic prospects of the city and region be clearly evident.

Brandon again found itself trying to catch up with Winnipeg. Perhaps finally recognizing that the capital city could not support an agricultural exhibition, the Winnipeg fair board decided in 1890 to offer an agricultural and industrial exhibition. This was to be the classic "booster" fair, with a healthy prize list, numerous special attractions, athletic competitions and displays of Winnipeg's industrial capacity. The first fair was held in 1891, and though Brandonites still uttered unfavorable reviews of Winnipeg's efforts, the larger urban exhibition had clearly outstripped Brandon's smaller effort. The local press took obvious delight in reporting that:

> During the latter part of last week the visitors from here to the Industrial Exhibition at Winnipeg began to return. Without exception they reported having the most disagreeable experience since coming to the country.

The writer went on to claim that were it not for the agricultural exhibits from Western Manitoba, the competitions would have been a disaster. The *Brandon Mail* registered its displeasure rather more graphically, commenting that:

> It is a pity Winnipeg has not adjourned its mongrel exhibition of fireworks and dogs.

This obvious disdain hid the fact that the Winnipeg Exhibition, by turning to industrial displays and more entertainment, had garnered unprecedented public support. It was a lesson the Brandon exhibition would soon learn.

FOLLOWING THE MOVE to a summer schedule in 1889, a change many other Manitoba fairs soon copied, the directors of the Brandon Agricultural Society sought ways of attracting a larger

9 *Board of Directors, Brandon fair, 1894.*
Front row, left to right: John McKellar, William Anderson, A. Kennedy, A.C. McPhail, James Gibson, Robert Matheson, Col. F.J. Clark, Alex Gamble. Back row: Thomas Jasper, W.N. Finlay, David Shiriff, (unidentified), William McKelvie, H.L. Patmore, R.E.A. Leech, Roderick McKenzie, W.H. Warner, John Hanbury, T. Horner, Peter Payne, T.B. Wallace, Henry Nicol, William Chalmers.

10 *Racing line-up prior to 1913.*

crowd while maintaining the integrity of the agricultural competitions. This meant adding games, sporting competitions, manufacturing displays and a variety of other enticements designed to broaden the exhibition's appeal. The change brought the fair into competition with other summer entertainments, like the circus and the Turf Club's regular schedule of races.

Fair-goers welcomed the improvements. Patrons no longer complained that the fair consisted of little more than vegetable displays and livestock judging. Initially, the additions consisted of amateur events, but soon enough the carnival circuit learned of the Brandon fair. In 1892, a Mr. Burrows brought several alligators as an attraction, and a man named Carswell charged a quarter to view his herd of domesticated deer. More enticing attractions followed. That same year, the *Brandon Mail* offered a delightful description of a game of chance held at the fair:

> We reached the enclosed table of Mr. Sid Squib. (There is no squib about him—he is a full charge). This table was perforated with numerous holes into which were thrust beautiful canes, cutting whips etc., and outside its low fence enclosure stood an anxious crowd waiting for their turn to purchase 25 cents worth of rings which were cautiously aimed at some coveted object on the perforated table. The game had no trickery and was most enjoyable. The outside boys captured some nice canes and cutting whips and Mr. Squib, the inside boy, secured many a stray quarter.

Though the agricultural parts of the fair continued to receive top billing—and rightly so, for the Brandon fair was clearly the best of the Manitoba exhibitions—the new attractions drew in the crowds. Rural folk and townspeople alike came in large numbers to see the exotic exhibits, to partake in the games of chance, and to thrill to the new entertainment acts brought in to add variety. In 1898, the exhibition schedule included the Three Zenos, a gymnastic act, the Austin Sisters, trapeze performers, Mademoiselle Aimee, the Human Fly, Miss Bessie Gilbert, a well known cornet player, the Royal Canadian Dragoons Musical Ride,

and a mammoth display of fireworks which were promised to "make a brilliant entertainment, such has never been placed before the public in Manitoba, and can only be surpassed at Toronto."

The exhibition directors also began to take much greater advantage of a long and friendly relationship with the Brandon Turf Club. The small but influential horse racing fraternity in Brandon had organized the Turf Club shortly after the city was established, built a small grandstand and offered a regular racing series. The club and the Brandon Agricultural Society had long recognized their common interests, and had often worked closely together to promote horse racing in western Manitoba. In 1884, for example, the Agricultural Society had raised $60 to support Turf Club activities. Horse racing had a sizable following in the Brandon area, as the large crowds at each meet attested, and the exhibition association was determined to tap into that interest. With the move to the summer fair, the fair directors added horse racing to their schedule, offering large purses in an effort to attract racing fans to the fair grounds. The years of cooperation with the Turf Club paid off; rather than resenting this intrusion into their area, the Turf Club instead assisted with the development of a top-notch racing card for the Brandon fair.

The early fair organization had been primarily concerned with agricultural development; but, by the 1890s, the exhibition association was interested in broadening its appeal. In 1892, the Western Agriculture and Arts Association was formally established, primarily to take over from the Brandon Agricultural Society. This modification was delayed, for reasons that are not altogether clear, for five years. The change was precipitated by the declining fortunes of the Brandon fair; even the shift to summer dates had not brought the annual celebration up to expectations. Further, in 1895, a huge Territorial Exhibition had been hosted in Regina, drawing competitors and exhibitors from across the West. On the positive side, arrangements with the Canadian Pacific Railway made it possible for exhibitors to stop for the Brandon fair at no extra charge, thus swelling the entry lists significantly. At the same time, talk of turning the Regina exhibition into an annual event challenged the Brandon association to put its own house in order.

IRONICALLY, THE MAJOR IMPETUS for change came out of Winnipeg, Brandon's arch-rival. The success of the capital city's new industrial and entertainment-based exhibition had not passed unnoticed, particularly given the flagging fortunes of the Brandon fair. The Western Agricultural and Arts Association (W.A.A.A.) specifically patterned itself on the Winnipeg Association. The Brandonites hoped to attract the same entertainment acts and carnival attractions that visited the Winnipeg show, expecting that they too could capitalize on the popularity and profitability of the entertainment extravaganza. It was unusual for a Brandon organization to model itself so carefully after a Winnipeg association; even more uncharacteristic were the generous offers of assistance and advice from the Winnipeg exhibition management.

The first regular meeting of the Western Agricultural and Arts Association was held on 26 February 1897. The new board of directors reflected the transformation of the Brandon exhibition, and of the city itself. S.D. Bedford, Superintendent of the Brandon Experimental Farm chaired the meeting. He was not the only agriculturalist present. W.J. Lindsay was a Brandon grain dealer and T.E. Kelly operated a livery stable. Most of the directors, however, represented the burgeoning business community. J.A. Christie was the manager of the Assiniboine Lumber Company, P. Payne owned the Beaubier House, J.W. Fleming was a druggist, William Ferguson was a wholesaler of liquor and cigars, and other members included an agent for Confederation Life, an engineer, a lawyer, a real estate agent, a bookkeeper and the owner of a planing mill. It was an impressive group, representing

11   Dr. S.A. Bedford, superintendent of the Experimental Farm, who forged a close link with the summer exhibition boards. He used the early fairs as a means of introducing to the farmers the results of research on grains and cattle.

They waved to friends preparing church booths for a week of lunches and dinners. Folding chairs and tables were being erected, foodstuffs delivered and stored, fuel for cookstoves was being stacked out of public view.

At the west doorway of the administration building there was a line-up of exhibitors waiting to register their entries. Tethered nearby in the parking lot were horses and cattle whose owners were in the office waiting to have stall numbers alloted.

In the display buildings salesmen could be seen polishing brand-new automobiles which had no dust on them, but which simply had to look better than the competing models across the aisle. Artists in crepe paper were fashioning the final rosettes and streamers as each local merchant attempted to out-do the other. Fair week was a time for competition, even in the commercial section.

But for drama, and a hint of things extra-ordinary, nothing could match the carnival crew. From pieces resembling the elements of a giant Tinker Toy set, sweating, swearing workmen assembled riding devices called the Rocket, the Octopus, the Caterpillar. Nearby, laborers pulled on the ropes, sailor-fashion, and canvas banners like sails rose in front of the sideshows, billowing in the breeze. Their

18

garish inscriptions promised
that inside the exhibition
visitors could see the biggest,
the smallest, the fattest,
the most bizarre.

Among the spectators
were some who had not
missed a "Scotchman's Day"
since boyhood. They could tell
stories of the setting-up of
Rubin and Cherry, or of the
Johnny J. Jones Exposition.
They remembered Jumbo, an
elephant owned by the Jones
Carnival, which was fitted
with a giant pad on his fore-
head so he could push
carnival wagons into location.

There were some who
over the years had come to
know key members of the
Royal American personnel.
These people knew that in
their lifetime they had seen
Leon Claxton, a heavy-set
black man, elevate himself
from roustabout to impresario,
the boss of Harlem in Havana.
In an earlier period Claxton
had drawn crowds for another
reason; he regularly competed
with gangs of men driving
five-foot, metal-tipped tent
stakes. Using only one arm,
and with a peculiar wind-
mill style, Claxton had been
an artist with the 16-pound
sledge.

continued

12 Exhibition Park early
in the century, with the new
cattle barn in centre back-
ground.

19

the best of the Brandon business community, but it was much different from the early boards.

The new group found itself facing a volatile situation almost immediately. D.M. McMillan, an acerbic character known for his sharp words and occasionally confrontational approach, was elected secretary-treasurer of the W.A.A.A. S.D. Bedford, president of the association, immediately tendered his resignation, although he was persuaded to hold it in abeyance until the next meeting. The *Brandon Mail* rose to McMillan's defense, noting that:

> It is true that in some of his ways he is a little brusque, but beneath that brusque exterior lies the very best of good nature and agreeableness.

Though few doubted his commitment to the city—he had previously been secretary-treasurer for Brandon—enough people disagreed with the selection to convince him to step down. On 22 April 1897, a second election was held, with Frank J. Clark winning the competition and the $300 a year salary that went with it. This internal matter laid to rest, the association could now turn to more pressing matters.

Though these men acknowledged the tremendous importance of agriculture to the regional economy, and worked consistently to further the industry, they were perhaps more aware than had been their predecessors of the importance of maintaining the interest of the townspeople in the annual exhibition.

The new board of directors was also rather more skilled at the cut and thrust of local and provincial politics. In Brandon, they seemed to find ready support for their grandiose plans for a major industrial and agricultural exhibition. City council promised $1,000 to assist the W.A.A.A. and transferred the land and buildings formerly owned by the Brandon Agricultural Society, valued at $4,000, to the new association. Even more impressive was the fact that local residents put up an additional $9,000. It was a notable accomplishment that augured well for the future.

ARMED WITH THIS REMARKABLE INDICATION of local support, the Western Agricultural and Arts Association took its case to the province. A delegation, consisting of J.A. Christie, John Hanbury, J.W. Fleming, Archie McPhail, William Lindsay, and two members of the provincial legislature, A.C. Fraser and Charles Adams, travelled to Winnipeg for meetings. The province had not always treated the Brandon fair well, or even equal to other exhibitions, and the new directors were determined to change that. They based their appeal on the promise to provide the best industrial and agricultural show the province had seen. The effort succeeded. With the support of Premier Thomas Greenway and Members of the provincial legislature from western Manitoba their request for $2,500 was approved.

The Western Agricultural and Arts Association still had a long way to go. They knew that the success of the agricultural components of their show depended very heavily on the size of their prize lists. Unable to provide enough funds themselves, they decided to petition surrounding communities for aid, an attempt that would serve as well to make the Brandon fair a truly Western Manitoba show. Anxious to avoid conflicts with neighboring towns, the W.A.A.A. even changed its dates a week to avoid overlapping with the smaller Carberry and Portage La Prairie fairs. Their efforts were rewarded, for in short order the Brandon fair had earned the enthusiastic support of the surrounding districts.

More work remained. Before 1897, the Brandon Fair had been a comparatively modest affair, held on a small 30 acre plot of land in the southern part of the city. This was not compatible with the extravagant plans of the Western Agricultural and Arts Association. After toying with the idea of moving the entire exhibition to a site closer to the actual townsite, they decided to remain in place and add to existing holdings. After the association had received formal title to the Brandon Agricultural Society's property, they promptly bought an additional 42 acres for the princely sum of $550.75.

A specialty of Scotchman's Day: the show must go on. Driving rain, windstorms, or heat that brought some livestock entries to prostration would never stop this crew. Like the couriers of whom Herodotus once wrote, who could not be stopped by rain or storm, or dark of night, carnival workers and their supporters were always on duty.

Cash-hungry exhibition directors once attempted to collect an admission charge on Scotchman's Day, offering a variety show as a sop for doing so. This practice was not to last, however, proof again that it is not wise to tamper with cherished traditions. Obvious question: who wants to see local talent when the imported variety is close at hand—and free?
Fred McGuinness

13   Homecraft section of the summer fair, 1899. This display was in the first Crystal Palace, destroyed in a cyclone in 1904.

21

14 *The "old" grandstand c. 1900.*

15 *Clydesdale stallions in judging ring at Brandon fair, 1898.*

Although the old site would do, the demands of the newly planned exhibition made the old facilities unsuitable. New buildings were required, outdated structures would have to go. It may be hard to appreciate the euphoria and excitement surrounding the W.A.A.A.'s plans for 1897, but for a city of some 4,400 souls it was excitement of the highest order.

The first order of business was a new grandstand. Before 1897, racing events had centered on the Turf Club's modest exhibition grounds racetrack. Now, a new facility was urgently needed. An agreement was quickly reached between the W.A.A.A. and the Turf Club, with the associations agreeing to split the costs of a new grandstand and half-mile track. In return, the Turf Club was granted free use of the track. The new facility reflected the vision of the exhibition promoters, for it ensured a first- class grandstand to complement what they hoped would be a first-class fair.

Much more had to be done before the grounds were ready. Other buildings, including a new stable, were erected. Directors travelled to Winnipeg to ensure that the attractions contracted for by the Winnipeg fair would come west to Brandon. Special attention was given to enlarging the prize lists, making sure that enough money was in the pot to attract farmers from all over western Manitoba and the Northwest Territories (not established as the separate provinces of Alberta and Saskatchewan until 1905). Special prizes, such as the $25.00 donated by the Imperial Bank for the best example of Red Fyfe wheat, and the plow donated by Massey Harris Company for the best heavy draught mare added luster to the growing number of prizes available for agricultural competitors. As in the past, special train rates were offered to fair visitors, making it easier for rural residents to afford the often lengthy and expensive journey to Brandon; it remained now for the exhibition directors to ensure a show that was worth the trip.

Never before had such effort gone into the planning of a Brandon fair, and never before had so much been at stake. The

🐚 *1899 3 August*
"The automobile or horseless carriage which Mr. and Mrs. Main rode in the circus procession last week, was the first ever seen in Brandon and was greatly admired."
from the *Brandon Independence.*

🐚 *1900 22 February*
"A Brandon poultry man whilst washing one of his birds for exhibition engaged in an argument with a competitor and the dispute waxed warm. He mastered his opponent's arguments but discovered that he had forgotten to take the hen out of the water, and that he was holding a dead bird."
from the *Brandon Independence.*

1897 exhibition represented Brandon's step into the big time. It was the city's attempt to join the growing number of industrial and agricultural fairs in Canada and to demonstrate that Brandon deserved a full share of the prosperity and investment flooding into the West in the midst of the post-1896 boom.

THE "BIG FAIR," as it quickly became known, found a ready and receptive audience. Even as opening day approached, one could see the difference from what went before. Large advertisements spoke of "The Great Holiday of the Year" and promised horse, foot and bicycle races, polo and football matches, and a huge fireworks display to commemorate Queen Victoria's Diamond Jubilee. There was scant mention of agriculture, though an impressive prize list and new facilities were designed to lure agricultural exhibitors off their farms. Particular attention was accorded the exciting attractions and carnival shows. Brandon had had its share of small acts in the past, but in 1897, the menagerie included the Fowler Brothers bicycling troupe, the Nelson Sisters aerial ladder act, the Flying Jordan Family and Barton's trick dogs. A highlight for many was Clara Beckwick's underwater act, which included eating, drinking and sewing while submerged in a tank.

Every effort was made to ensure that nothing was left out. Mrs. Stripp's 300 seat eatery—housed in a tent—made sure no one suffered through want of food. Machinery and implement displays filled the grounds. Displays of women's work filled part of the exhibition hall, giving the homemakers of western Manitoba ample opportunity to prove their skills in culinary crafts, sewing, knitting and artwork. Displays of school work, including special presentations from the Qu'Appelle Indian School and Wasbakada Indian Home at Elkorn, demonstrated the accomplishments of the region's young scholars. A seemingly endless series of baseball games, football matches, track events and horse races thrilled the

᷃❧ *1904 20 August*
"*When on May 28th the old main building went into kindling wood before the vagaries of a wandering cyclone, it left free an excellent site for a larger, more pretentious and more up-to-date building, and with characteristic western enterprise the association grappled with the problem of erecting this new building before fair time. The task was a large one, but save for a few finishing touches about the dome the work was completed by the time the exhibition opened. This new structure cost upwards of $15,000. The grounds are nicely located, are arranged and planted with a view to increasing their beauty, and each year will add to their attractiveness.*"
from the *NorWest Farmer*.

16   *New Crystal Palace, built in 1904.*

25

large grandstand crowds. Local horsemen and athletes often faced stiff competition from "outsiders" brought in to enliven the proceedings and the fight for the substantial cash rewards.

The competitions, whether agricultural, athletic, or involving women's work, all had the glorification of accomplishment as their central theme. The purpose of the 1897 fair, like those before and those after, was to select the best from farm, sporting ground and kitchen. The winners became king or queen for a day. To the victor of the athletic events went a year's worth of bragging rights and a cash prize. To the cattleman, grain grower or vegetable producer, the fame attached to winning in Manitoba's best agricultural show carried invaluable commercial benefits, to say nothing of the pride of accomplishment. Similarly, the lady who walked away with the ribbon for the best loaf of bread had demonstrated her superior skill to thousands of other women and men.

The Big Western Fair had tapped just the right vein. Crowds estimated at more than 10,000 attended on a single day, proving that the fair directors' enthusiastic predictions were not far wrong. Local businessmen, many of whom offered special fair-time deals, praised the results as their cash registers rang up record sales. The town's hotels were filled to capacity and, as before, the exhibition association helped to connect visitors with townspeople willing to provide room and board during the week.

People from Brandon and particularly the surrounding district came in droves to the fair grounds; the small town of Hartney sent more than 150 on a single day and other centres showed similar enthusiasm. The combination of agricultural competitions, ladies' work displays, sporting events and the much loved carnival proved irresistible. The fair had promised a holiday, and a great community party, and it delivered. The fair association had offered its show as a replacement for the round of small local fairs, arguing that a combined effort would generate a much better result than a series of minor exhibitions. The results strongly suggested that they were right. Brandon's exhibition had become the number one regional show.

17   *Merry-go-round at Brandon Fair in the early 1900's.*

THE 1897 EXHIBITION MARKED A MAJOR TURNING POINT for the Brandon fair. The change was more than cosmetic, more than just the addition of a new name. The Western Agricultural and Arts Association had much different goals and ambitions than did its more modest predecessors. Partly out of a desire to put Brandon on the map, partly because the urban boosters wanted a fair they could sell to townsfolk and farmers alike, and partly out of a simple interest in staging a grand show, the directors of the W.A.A.A. opted for a more modern and more urban exhibition. Their gamble paid off, and the future prospects of the Brandon summer fair looked extremely bright.

The summer exhibition built on its success. Although there were occasional problems with the weather—a curse for all the summer shows—healthy crowds, hundreds of exhibitors and handsome profits for the association pointed to the continuing support for the Western Fair, Big Summer Fair, Western Manitoba's Big Fair, or, as it was called after 1908, the Inter-Provincial Exhibition. From 1897 to 1912, the exhibition continued much the same, growing in size and fame but retaining the familiar mix of entertainment and agriculture.

Carnival shows and midways came to dominate the annual presentation. The advertising each year touted a mysterious and startling collection of exotic delights, athletic feats, and musical or dance ensembles. Who could fail to thrill at the performance of Lockart's Troupe of Trained Elephants on display in 1903 or the International Congress of Strongmen who had presented their "Samsonian feats" the previous year?

Finding the right kind and number of fair attractions proved difficult, particularly as Brandon was rather isolated from the main entertainment areas of North America. Typically, a committee of directors was delegated to visit several American cities, review the stage acts available for the summer fair circuit and sign an appropriate group for the Brandon fair. Selecting a few headline performers still left a major part of the preparations undone, as

1906 21 July
Rev. Mr. McIntyre and Rev. Mr. Munroe addressed the board meeting of WAAA to urge that for the good name of the association, the city, and the citizens, that the directors do all in their power to prevent gambling, and the performance of lewd shows during the fair. Members of the hotel association asked at the same meeting that the illicit sale of intoxicants be prohibited upon the exhibition gounds.
from the minutes.

1906 Exhibition Week
During exhibition week, the board of directors debated the motion, be it resolved that "the side show 'The Girl From Up There,' be closed, the same being obnoxious and contrary to the rules of the association." Motion carried.

18   *Early ferris wheel, prior to 1913.*

the necessary melange of games, sideshows and rides still had to be assembled. Initially, such attractions were contracted on an individual basis. In 1908, a Mr. Oppenheimer was given a contract to organize and coordinate the midway events, although the agreement was not honored. The next year, the Parker Amusement Company, which regularly toured the American midwest, came to Brandon. Anxious to place the carnival aspects on a more regular footing, the exhibition contracted with this firm in 1910 to provide a complete midway. These arrangements, combined with the addition of moving rides like the merry-go-round and a slip-the-slip, brought the Brandon summer fair in line with other larger scale urban exhibitions. Brandon was moving into the big time, reaping the benefits of joining the circuit of large fairs but also experiencing the detrimental effects of that association.

The problems emerged quickly as big-city hucksters followed the western Canada fair circuit to Brandon. Sideshows attracted particular attention, as eager fair-goers gathered outside the canvas tents lining the "pike," egged on by the smooth-tongued pitch-men to part with a few cents and witness some extraordinary natural wonder. And who could resist such tantalizing delights as "Millie-Christien," a 'double-woman' on view at the 1902 exhibition. One cynical newspaperman noted the obvious interest:

> At every performance a number were allowed to examine the curiosity and all pronounced it "the real thing." After the show had pulled its tent pegs and left the exhibition grounds, it is said that a strange transformation in Millie Christien took place, whereby she or they were able to navigate alone. No doubt Millie and Christien will grow together in time for the next show.

The sideshows, proof positive that P.T. Barnum's adage "There is a sucker born every minute" is only too true, remained a positive feature. Most knew the shows were fake, that the promised feats or touted deformities were artificial, but the draw nonetheless remained irresistible.

The shows flirted with the risque and the illegal. Front-men, their faces contorted in lewd grins, winked at their audiences of young men and invited them to view a scandalous display of hootchy-kootchy girls. Few could resist a quick visit to the exotic flesh-pots of the Orient or Arabia that the hucksters promised. Unscrupulous gamblers also followed the fair circuits, hoping to capitalize on the naivete of the small-town folk gathered for the event. Games of chance, card matches and bets on the various races and competitions were freely, though discreetly, available. The card shark or bookie was always ready, at the first sight of an exhibition official or police officer, to fold up his game and meld back into the swarming throngs on the fair grounds.

Exhibition directors and city officials fought each year to keep the undesirable elements under control. It was a losing battle. The gamblers and burlesque operators were ever-present, often promising to clean up their acts but only too willing to put on special, "private" showings for the extremely eager after hours or when surveillance had dropped. More importantly, they were simply providing what the farmers and townsfolk who visited the fair wanted to see. As one commentator correctly, if sheepishly, pointed out:

> Who of the male population that visits the fair fails to "do" the pike? It's like going up to the bar and not asking for a drink, isn't it? We generally understand that we're being done, too, but somehow we seem to take pleasure in the fact. Barnum often remarked that the people simply loved to be humbugged, and the large majority of us amply bear out his statement.

That the young men seemed to enjoy being fleeced did not sit well with local reform and church groups. Organizations like the Moral and Reform Council of Brandon regularly petitioned the exhibition to eliminate the unsavory elements from what was touted as a family show. In 1905, a broad attack was leveled at the Brandon and Winnipeg exhibitions for their undesirable

19 *Pipers lead the livestock parade in front of the grandstand some time prior to 1913.*

20 *A bird's-eye view of the Brandon fairgrounds, 1904.*

21 *Indian pow-wows, displays, and encampments were a popular feature of early fairs. At the summer fair board meeting of 8 April 1911 directors were advised of a letter from Ottawa in which the Department of Indian Affairs requested that the board discontinue the practice of encouraging pagan Indians from congregating at the fair.*

29

attractions. The *Nor'West Farmer* criticized the fairs for the blatant sexuality of several of the sideshows:

> Scantily dressed females were announced by lewd men who openly stated to the crowd that these "ladies" — (what a libel on the name!) would give an exhibition for men. Ladies and Sunday School teachers, they said, were not invited.

The men and boys of the west, the paper continued, were not ready for the terrible moral shock such shows induced.

The criticism continued, and was quickly broadened to include gambling on the grounds and the illegal sale of intoxicating liquors. In 1908, Mayor Clement and Alderman Middleton did not even wait for the exhibition to act, moving on their own to close down certain concessions and attractions which they deemed objectionable. The exhibition tried to combat the infiltration of illicit acts. An agreement was reached with city council whereby the City of Brandon paid for extra police protection during the fair. Similarly, the amusements committee was empowered to investigate the various shows and close down any that violated the directors' sense of propriety. In 1906, for example, a side show called "The Girl From Up There" was closed on the grounds that it was obnoxious and contrary to the rules of the association.

THE FAIR HAD MUCH MORE to offer than the midway. Each year, more and more manufacturers applied for display space, anxious to capitalize on the large assembly of farmers and ranchers. The exhibition brought in a large number of special features, often providing the citizens of western Manitoba with their first glimpse of new technology. Exhibits of new farm machines always attracted special interest, as did such unique features as a moving picture show highlighting the Boer War and Queen Victoria's funeral which played to large audiences during the 1901 fair. For a number of years, the exhibition also played host to the North West Mounted Police, who thrilled the crowds with their presentation of tent-pegging, revolver-shooting and musical rides. The crowd took particular delight in regular tug-of-war competitions between the police and local men, particularly when the farmers out-pulled the mounties.

Numerous attempts were made to increase attendance and to spice up proceedings. The exhibition invited hundreds of natives to camp on the grounds, counting on their traditional dress and tepees to serve as a major attraction. The helpful cooperation of city council resulted in the declaration in 1908 of a Citizen's Day, with a half-day holiday scheduled to coincide with a day of special events at the fair grounds. The Ladies Hospital Aid helped both their cause and the exhibition by offering an impressive Hospital Tea Room, where fair-goers could find a complete meal at a reasonable price, with proceeds targeted for improvements to the local hospital. Care was taken not to ignore local residents in the celebrations. In 1907, for example, a special "Old Boys" day was held, honoring the early pioneers of western Manitoba and inviting all to participate in a reunion at the exhibition grounds.

Parades also emerged in this early period as an important and extremely popular part of the annual fair. In 1912, the association declared the fourth day of the exhibition, 23 July, as "Travellers Day." The central feature of the festivities was a "monster" parade, which snaked through the downtown area before heading back to the exhibition grounds. Home-owners along the parade route were invited to decorate their houses, with a prize of $25.00 offered for the best design. The parade itself contained seventeen separate sections, including floats by labor groups, municipalities, manufacturers, wholesalers, retail stores, and many others, plus 12 marching bands. The citizens of Brandon had never before witnessed such a mobile extravaganza, and flocked by the hundreds to line the parade route. Though the "Travellers Parade" did not immediately become an annual event, in a few years it would become an integral feature of the exhibition.

✑ *1907 30 November*
The board today received 16 applications for the position of secretary-treasurer. They approved the application of Mr. Fraser, who agreed to take the position for $1,000 per annum.

BRANDON --- AUGUST 9, 10, 11, 12.

Western Manitoba's Big Fair

THE AGRICULTURAL FAIR OF THE WEST — "IF YOU MISS IT YOU'LL REGRET IT"

GREAT EXHIBITION OF THE PRODUCTS OF THIS GREAT COUNTRY

GRAND ATTRACTIONS.

Musical Rides and Military Sports.

By the North West Mounted Police.

Exciting Speeding Events.

Hurdle Races, Team Races, $1000.00 Free-for-All.

Magnificent Displays of Fireworks.

Including "Living Pictures in Fireworks," and the "Bombardment of Alexandria.

REDUCED RAILWAY RATES good for the WEEK of the FAIR and SPECIAL DAILY EXCURSIONS.

Increased Accommodation —Room for All.

FOR ALL PARTICULARS AND PRIZE LISTS WRITE TO

R. M. MATHESON, President.　　　**F. J. CLARK**, Manager, Brandon, Man.

22　*A "Big Fair" advertisement from the Nor'West Farmer, 5 July 1904.*

1908 24 March

On this date, A. C. McPhail, vice-president of the Brandon fair, officially known as the Western Agricultural and Arts Association of Manitoba, wrote to the MP, Hon. Clifford Sifton.

This hand-written letter was to change exhibition history in western Manitoba.

"Mr. Sifton, Dear Sir: Some time ago the Fair Board here asked me to write you to see if there was any possibility of Brandon securing the Dominion Fair in the near future, no doubt you know all the advantages that Brandon possesses better than I could set them forth. I think we can put up as good an exhibit of stock, especially horses, as can be got in the Dominion, and Brandon would show what the farmers in these western plains can accomplish as well if not better than most others. We have I think the best grounds for a fair that lies west of Ontario.

It is not necessary for me to try to add anything as you know the feeling, here and now it would be appreciated if we could secure the Dominion Fair for one year and incidentally the grant of $50,000 which accompanies it. Yours, etc, (signed) A.C. McPhail,

This letter recently came to light when Dr. Lee Clark, MP for Brandon-Souris, found it among the Sifton papers.

The show had changed a great deal from the small agricultural exhibition hosted before 1897. The break, though, was more apparent than real. When planning the first of the "Big" fairs in 1897, the exhibition directors recognized the marketing limitations of an agricultural show. To garner the attendance necessary for financial success, it was necessary to attract large crowds and take a percentage of the revenue from midways, side shows and grandstand performances. In 1909, the directors piously declared that "It has always been the policy to make the agricultural features the leading ones, with the amusements and attractions a secondary consideration." While that may have been their intent, it was clear the crowds came more for the midway than the horse judging, more for the "freak" shows than the displays of ladies work. As the *Brandon Sun* noted in 1912:

> It is essentially a farmers' fair, but to those uninterested in the production of world-famous livestock this fair always has sufficient drawing power in the matter of fairway attractions.

The Brandon summer fair was, fundamentally, an agricultural show, though all the hoopla and advertising might suggest otherwise. The exhibition directors went out of their way to highlight the best products of farm and field. The prize lists offered in each category were genuinely impressive, and continued to grow every year. The association took pride in the number of competitors and the high quality of their winners. Competitors at the Brandon fair frequently continued on to other regional exhibitions, and occasionally to such important national events as the Winter Fair in Toronto.

The association did not stint in making farmers welcome at the annual fair. Negotiations with railway companies ensured that fair-goers paid the lowest possible price for their excursion to the exhibition. When the Great Northern Railway reached Brandon shortly after the turn of the century, farmers who previously had been unable to visit the fair could attend in large numbers. The

Brandon show could reach even further afield: In 1908, for instance, great delight was expressed in the large number of Dakotans planning to attend. By 1911, the list of excursions was extremely impressive. Canadian Pacific Railway ran excursion trains from Broadview, Carman, MacGregor, Arcola, Birtle, Miniota, Winnipeg, Cupar, Estevan, Lenore and Lyleton. Canadian Northern offered trips from Carman and Dauphin and the Great Northern Railway departed from St. John and Devils Lake, North Dakota. All of the trains stopped at intermediate points as well. In addition, persons travelling from even further away received reduced fares.

Providing lodging for the massive influx of rural visitors posed yet another dilemma. Knowing that the hotels would fill quickly each year, the association appealed to local residents to open their homes—for a fee of course—to fair-goers. Brandon College, in the midst of summer vacation, opened its doors to visitors while the fair was on. The effort was smashingly successful. Hasty preparations in 1906 secured rooms for over six hundred. In 1910, the association claimed to have provided temporary accommodation for some three thousand visitors, no mean accomplishment in a town of only 13,000 citizens. Those people who had room, but no bedding, were provided with the required materials. For those who were concerned about the quality of potential boarders, the association soothingly promised, "There will be no danger of undesirable people being sent to you. The bureau will be especially careful of this."

It clearly required a total town effort to ensure that the fair visitors were comfortable and welcome. The special arrangements for farmers continued at the fair grounds. The machinery exhibits provided farmers with their first glimpse of new agricultural technology. When developers of the new mechanical tractors sought to bring their product to market, it was not surprising that they moved first to the agricultural fairs, like the Brandon show. The gas-powered machines were still novelties in the pre-war West, and the exhibition went out of its way to introduce the farmers to

* è▲ 1908 17 July*
The board of WAAA today decried the action of Mayor Clement and Alderman Middleton in ordering the closing of certain concessions and the arrest of the owners. It was moved and seconded that, "This board place on record their regret at the hasty action of Mayor Clement and Alderman Middleton at visiting the Fair Grounds and ordering the closing of certain concessions on the Grounds." Carried.

è▲ 1911 8 April
The directors learned in a letter from Ottawa that the Department of Indian Affairs wants the exhibition to discontinue the practice of encouraging pagan Indians to congregate at the fair, and that in the future no concession of any kind was to be granted to them.

è▲ 1911 5 August
Foul play was confirmed in the death of two horses. They had died due to poisoning by strychnine. The board passed this information along to the crown attorney for immediate attention.

the technology. The 1912 fair included a grand agricultural parade of gas and oil tractors, steam engines, separators, plows and portable machinery. A heavy downpour spoiled the effect, as the machines bogged down in the mud of the race track, but the attempt to put the future of agriculture on parade was undoubtedly appreciated.

THE NURTURING OF PRAIRIE AGRICULTURE continued throughout the grounds and inside the exhibition buildings. In 1910-1911, the federal government nursery at Indian Head, Saskatchewan established an exhibition plantation to promote the planting of trees. The Dominion Experimental Farm staff put on several displays, including a presentation from the Brandon farm, and fruit and vegetable products from the government of British Columbia. In 1900, C. Braithwaite, Weed Inspector for the Province of Manitoba, hosted a display of more than 90 noxious weeds, and was kept busy answering numerous questions from concerned farmers on the identification and control of these hated enemies. The assistance from the various governments ensured that each year the exhibition had much to offer in the educational line.

The exhibition also took advantage of the proximity of Brandon Experimental Farm to promote innovation in agriculture. The fair and the farm had a long and friendly relationship, but never more so than during fair time. In addition to the Experimental Farm's exhibition display, the fair board established regular carriage trips from the fair grounds to the farm. Visiting farmers had ample opportunity to learn about new seeds, improved sowing techniques and harvesting practices. By assisting this educational process, the exhibition was only fulfilling its primary function, that of promoting the development of agriculture.

Of course, there was no better example of this constant effort than the agricultural competitions themselves. Though city folks often lost sight of the intense battles being waged in the show-ring or at the judges' tables, the exhibition events were of vital importance to the farmers. Livestock breeders watched the results anxiously, for carrying off the prize ribbon for Shorthorns, Angus, Herefords, Holsteins, Jersey or Ayrshires meant a great deal in the marketing of one's herd. The range of agricultural events at each year's fair was stunning. In addition to the high-profile cattle and horse-judging competitions, there were hundreds of entries in the sheep, swine, poultry, grains, and dairy produce events.

The purpose was simple. By putting the best agricultural produce in the land on display—and each year entries arrived in Brandon from further and further away—the exhibition was highlighting the accomplishments of the country's farmers and cattle breeders. The exhibition symbolized the accomplishments and potential of the region, and encouraged all agriculturalists to strive towards higher standards. It was more than a matter of personal accomplishment, more than a glorification of individual talent; the fair brought out the pride of the land, and exhibited it so all could share in the reflected glory of the country's best farmers and cattlemen.

The high stakes ensured some memorable competitions, and hot debates over the judges' decisions—and not infrequently over the quality of the judges themselves. The 1900 Clydesdale stallion competition, for example, pitted Winnipeg champion Pilgrim against the local favorite, Erskine Lad. The decision in favour of Erskine Lad was roundly cheered by the crowd, who delighted in yet another victory over a Winnipeg challenger.

It would have been hard for a fair-goer in the early 20th century to make sense of the mixture of sights, sounds and smells which assaulted his senses upon entering the grounds. The scattered array of buildings, alluring tents of the sideshows, children's laughter echoing through the grounds from the midway rides, the aromas wafting from the Ladies Hospital Aid Tea Room and other food concessions, the lusty cheers rising from the grandstand as thousands rose as one to cheer during the stretch run, the clanging mechanical noises from the equipment display,

1912 31 August
Sheriff Henderson advised the directors of WAAA that in view of the scarcity of labor, a number of prisoners now in the jail could be provided to assist with the concrete work on the new grandstand. The directors agreed to provide transportation and their noon-time meal.

1912 21 December
Mr. McPhail advised the directors of WAAA that in his opinion the new grandstand should have a "lock-up," so that offenders when arrested could be kept in preference to sending all of them downtown.

23 *Captain F.J. Clark, manager of the Western Agricultural and Arts Association of Manitoba. Between 1897 and 1907 he is credited with raising the status of Brandon's fair to the point that it was one of Canada's largest. Brandon's was one of the first fairs to attract a crowd of over 10,000 in a single day.*

36

and a potpourri of other elements combined in a mysterious fashion to transport the fair-goers from the harsh realities of everyday to a world of fantasy and enchantment. It was too much to see at once; the constant distractions and the pull of many features turned one around in circles, trying to find a place to start, hoping to never have to leave. Like all good fairs, there was something for everyone, and it seemed at times as though everyone was there.

On busy days, crowds estimated at 20,000 jammed the fair grounds; and total attendance was typically estimated in the tens of thousands for the five or six day event. The attendance helped, for adults paid $.50 each to enter to the grounds, and the revenue put the exhibition association on a firm financial footing, even after covering the heavy expenses for constructing new facilities and obtaining new attractions. In 1912, the association announced with considerable pride that all outstanding loans, including a number from the long-suffering exhibition directors, had been repaid. Even better, the bank book recorded a hefty $11,000 surplus. The path from 1892 to 1912 had been a shaky one, but all the signs pointed to a secure and bright future for the Inter-Provincial Exhibition.

THAT THE FAIR PROCEEDED as quickly and expeditiously as it did in its first twenty years was largely due to the hard work and innovative ideas of its managers. Frank J. Clark, then a young, aggressive man just out from Winnipeg, had been selected as secretary-treasurer in 1897. This position effectively made him the manager of the fair, responsible for the day-to-day details. Clark performed his job admirably, a fact well recognized by the board and others involved with the fair. Feeling that his efforts were not being sufficiently rewarded financially, Clark approached the exhibition board in January 1907 with a request for a salary of $2,400. When he was turned down, he tendered his resignation. The board then called for applications, noting that they wanted some-

one who would provide office space, clerical assistance, and who would work full time for three months and on call for the balance of the year.

There was no shortage of applicants. Six men asked for the job, offering their services for salaries ranging from $1,750 to $2,200. After withdrawing discreetly to discuss the matter, the board decided to offer the position to Mr. Clark at his requested salary. By the fall of 1907, Clark had reconsidered, and again tendered his resignation. Yet another competition was held, this time resulting in the selection of Mr. C. Fraser as manager, at a salary of $1,000 per year.

Charles Fraser's tenure proved to be rather brief. Just before the 1909 exhibition, he officially resigned. Though exhibition records do not indicate the reason for his resignation, it generated a heated discussion. Former manager Frank Clark stormed out of the meeting in protest, offering his own resignation (subsequently withdrawn) from the exhibition board in the process. The *Brandon Sun* was upset with the change and commented:

> Charles Fraser is the man who was instrumental in getting the Brandon exhibition into such shape as to deserve this praise. The Fair board directors will do well to consider carefully the matter before losing the services of a man who has made good. The interests of the exhibition and the city demand it.

The support did little good for Fraser. After asking him to stay on to complete the books for 1909, the exhibition board refused to pay him, an action which led to a short-lived lawsuit.

The departure of Fraser raised again the matter of hiring a manager. Frank Booth was appointed as acting secretary-treasurer while the association searched for a replacement. This time, 16 men applied for the post. It was finally offered to W.I.Smale, who had initially joined the board in 1906 as an associate director for the Carberry Summer Fair. Smale was operating a business in Carberry at the time, but he promised to sell out by the spring of 1910 and take up his $1,800-a-year post. The choice turned out to be a propitious one, for Smale would emerge in short order as the driving force behind the exhibition, responsible for some of its grandest dreams and greatest accomplishments.

THOUGH THE SUMMER FAIR HAD EMERGED as the biggest single attraction in the Brandon and western Manitoba area, it was not alone in promoting agricultural excellence. The City of Brandon hosted not one, but two agricultural extravaganzas, both noted as leaders in their respective fields. The second, of course, was the Brandon Winter Fair.

The idea was not new to Brandon, but was again a time honored tradition carried from the Old World and Ontario by the early settlers of the prairie West. It was also a very different concept than the summer exhibition. Winter fairs were often limited to cattle sales, though it was not uncommon for judging competitions to be attached to the auctions. The purpose, therefore, was primarily to promote the sale of livestock and to encourage improvement in breeding lines and care of animals.

The idea first emerged in Brandon from the fertile mind of Alderman J.W. Sifton in 1884. He suggested the establishment of a quarterly series of "cattle fairs" which would provide local cattlemen with an opportunity to sell their stock in a competitive atmosphere. The logic was simple. The experience with the wheat economy in the 1880s demonstrated the dangers of relying on a single crop for regional stability. It was hoped that city support for the livestock industry would encourage diversification of the regional economy.

The first Brandon winter fair was held on 23 December 1884, in the buildings of A. Harrison and Company. There were some complaints with this first effort, particularly about scheduling the event so close to Christmas. Alexander Griswold, drawing on experience from numerous fat stock fairs in Ontario, wondered why the fair organizers emphasized breeding stock, and not fat

stock ready for the butcher. Only if the latter were highlighted, he claimed, would the farmers take the time to bring in their cattle for auction.

The plan seemed to have had modest success, and several shows were scheduled for the following year. There was not sufficent support to sustain a lasting effort and the Brandon show effort faded, leaving other centres like Winnipeg and Portage La Prairie to push ahead. However, cattlemen and horse breeders were not about to let the idea die. Groups like the South Western Stock Association, formed in 1883, and the more influential western branch of the Livestock Association, headed by R.J. Collins and Frank Russell, continued to push the development of a western Manitoba livestock industry.

The horsebreeders were not to be left out. J.D. McGregor and several others like John E. Smith, Dan McCaig, Webb Bowen and W.E. Huston had long since established Brandon as one of the most important stallion centres in North America, referred to by its boosters as the "Horse Capital of Canada." Understandably, they too sought a market to display their stock and to compete against each other. A Spring Stallion Show had been started in 1891, but the horsemen sought a larger audience and better facilities for their important competitions. As early as 1904, J.D. McGregor had petitioned Brandon city council for support for a winter fair.

That effort failed, but in 1906, a number of Brandon businessmen, politicians and farm representatives decided to organize the city's first full-scale Winter Fair. No one expected that this preliminary effort would prove such a smashing success. Few agriculturalists could afford to miss an event that promised the first Provincial Spring Stallion Show, a Seed Grain Fair, a School of Stock Judging, a Poultry Show, and the annual meetings of the Cattle Breeders' Association, Sheep and Swine Breeders Association, Horse Breeders' Association, Canadian Seed Growers Association and the Grain Growers' Association.

24 *J.D. McGregor, director, past-president, winter fair's moving force.*

25 *A sale of stallions, city hall grounds, 8th Street and Princess Avenue, Brandon, before the construction of the winter fair buildings. Sales of horses and cattle were held on the city hall grounds before the winter fair buildings were erected. This sale of stallions was conducted when Brandon was known as "The Horse Capital of Canada."*

26 *Seventh Annual Convention of the Grain Growers Association meeting in Brandon, December, 1909.*

40

Organizers scrambled to make arrangements. They appealed to the townspeople of Brandon to provide accommodation for the hundreds of visitors expected. The Winter Fair did not have its own facilities, but arranged with the Western Canada Flour Mills Company for use of their judging ampitheatre and second-floor rooms. The seed fair was held close by in the Kelly Building while the horse show was staged on the grounds of City Hall. The city council was asked to provide some form of entertainment, preferably a "smoker" with a musical program. The event was open to the public free of charge.

THE ADDITION OF A WINTER FAIR was greeted with enthusiasm by the directors of the Brandon Summer Fair. Far from being in competition, board members viewed the late February—early March presentation as complementary to the summer event. F.J. Clark, secretary-treasurer of the summer fair, was also secretary of the winter fair. The cooperation went one step further. In 1905, the Western Agricultural and Arts Association had considered developing its own seed fair as a special attraction. Because the winter fair was a more appropriate time for the show, the summer fair board not only passed on the idea to its winter partner, but also provided a generous prize list to ensure healthy competition. Though the two organization remained separate, they had in this first instance established a friendly, cooperative relationship that would last for many years.

The event was a resounding success. Hundreds of people attended, the lectures and educational displays were lauded by all, and the organizers agreed that this initial effort had been amply justified. There were 58 entries in the Seed Grain Fair and 247 competitors in the Poultry Show. They were particularly pleased with the response to the horse show, where the 37 entries delighted the large and enthusiastic crowds. Such notable stallions as Cairnhill, a Clydesdale owned by the Brandon Horse Company, and Perpetual Motion, shown by W.H. Bryce of Arcola, carried off top honors. Flushed with this success, the winter fair board began to plan for future shows.

The first concern was securing suitable quarters. Operating the Winter Fair out of loaned warehouse space simply would not do. Winter Fair chairman John Inglis, and executive members W.J. Lindsay, D. Shirriff, J.P. Brisbin, A. McKenzie, P. Middleton and Joseph Cornell, together with manager F. Clark, petitioned city council for financial support. Their request received a boost in late March 1906 when promoters S.C. Doran and James Smith brought forward a proposal for a large permanent structure, including a judging arena, horse exchange and feeding stable at the corner of Princess and Thirteenth. City council agreed to pay $250 for the use of the facilities for ten days each year.

The plans fell through, and when the crowds gathered for the second Winter Fair in February 1907, they met at the Hughes block on the west side of Tenth Street. A large civic reception at St. Matthew's Hall touched off the event, which attracted sizable crowds—up to twelve hundred in a single day. The Cattle Breeders, meeting again at Brandon, made a decision crucial to the survival of the Winter Fair. Over the protests of some cattlemen from the Winnipeg area, they agreed to make the Brandon Winter Fair the site of their annual stock sale, thus ensuring the continuation of a prominent and popular feature.

The obvious interest in the undertaking spurred the organizers to make the event more permanent. Early in 1907, a joint stock company known as the Brandon Winter Fair and Livestock Association (B.W.F.L.A.) was formed. Stock subscriptions were called for by new president, J.D. McGregor, and a decision was made to purchase a block of land at 10th and McTavish. With the solid backing of the local business community, the directors were able to let a contract for a $40,000 exhibition building to house the yearly event. In addition, the B.W.F.L.A. arranged for livestock groups to use the facility for regular cattle shows, ensuring more frequent use of the structure.

27 *First winter fair board, 1908. Left to right, James McQueen, J.D. McGregor, president, Joseph Cornell, O.L. Harwood, Robert Hall, Charles Fraser, W. Warren, (unidentified), G.R. Coldwell.*

28 *Market held in winter fair building, 1913.*

29 *The Manitoba Winter Fair Building, 1910.*

The format for the 1908 winter fair remained as before, though the commodious new building, erected under the careful attentions of architect W.A. Elliott, provided premium display and exhibition space. There were general plaudits for the fair management and particular delight taken in the keen competitions in the show ring. Most of those attending spoke very highly of the numerous educational opportunities available at the fair. As in the summer show, displays by government agencies, implement dealers and other manufacturers attracted great attention. In addition, a series of lectures and meetings of breed associations and other agricultural groups created a very business-like atmosphere for the entire proceedings. As before, the horses attracted the most attention, and entries like Sir William Van Horne's grand champion Clydesdale, Lord Ardwall, James McKirdy's Canadian and Manitoba-bred Champion, Lord Gartly, brought in from Napinka stole the spotlight.

THE BRANDON WINTER FAIR had been set on a solid foundation. Local residents, farmers and cattlemen all lauded the annual presentations. Said Fred Stone of the *Brandon Sun*,

> It is worth more to Brandon than half a dozen spasmodic, pin-head publicity campaigns.

The winter fair garnered support from many quarters. The federal government provided a handsome $1,000 to assist the association, numerous companies and clubs offered cash prizes or trophies for the competitions, and city council maintained its aid to the valuable promotion.

Like the summer fair, the winter exhibition directors had large dreams and sought to establish their show as the province's preeminent winter event. On the heels of the 1908 winter fair, board members J.D. McGregor, Andrew Graham and Charles Fraser established a Provincial Winter Fair and Fat Stock Association to further their ambitions. The establishment of this second organization meant there were then two separate, but related groups associated with the winter fair. The B.W.F.L.A. was primarily a land-holding company, responsible for the management and financing of the winter fair buildings. The second organization, soon renamed the Manitoba Winter Fair and Livestock Association, actually organized the annual show. Though formal designation of the Brandon show as a Provincial Winter Fair did not follow, the directors need not have worried. Theirs was the premier agricultural event in the province, after the Brandon Summer Fair of course, and their impressive lists of prizes, patrons and competitors was enough to rattle any would-be rival.

The mounting success of the Winter Fair was interrupted in 1911. The razing of the Brandon Mental Asylum the previous fall left hundreds of inmates homeless. At the request of the provincial government, the winter fair board surrendered their facilities. The gesture was greatly appreciated, but it left the fair without a home. The Summer Fair board offered the use of its facilities, and the horse, cattle, sheep and swine competitions were held at the summer fair grounds. The poultry exhibit, vegetable displays and the seed grain fair were held in the Armory closer to downtown. The standard fare of lectures and speeches were slated for City Hall.

The management did the best it could given the obvious limitations. The Canadian National Railway ran its suburban train to the summer fair grounds throughout the days of the show. Special admission prices of $.25 for a single admission or $1.50 for a season ticket, both of which included the train fare, were offered to entice spectators.

Fair manager W.I. Smale, who like F.J. Clarke held a similar post with the summer fair, did a marvelous job of handling the unwieldy arrangements. A record number of entries were received in various categories, and the competition was again first-rate.

There was particular attention given to the extensive list of educational speakers arranged for the show. A talk by Miss A.B. Juniper of the Manitoba Agricultural College on the advantages

30 *On the evening of 5 November, 1910, fire destroyed the Brandon Mental Hospital.*

31 *Following the fire which destroyed the mental hospital, the patients walked to the winter fair buildings where they were accommodated as the hospital was being re-built.*

45

32 *Glencarnock Victor, J.D. McGregor's herd sire, in 1912 won the grand championship at the Chicago International Livestock Exposition.*

and prospects of Household Science, an address by Dominion commissioners W.A. Dryden and W.T. Ritch on the prospects of the Sheep Industry, James Murray's discussion on growing and feeding alfalfa, a lecture by Dominion Agriculturalist J.H. Grisdale on improving agricultural conditions and a discussion by Harold Orchard of Lintrathen, Manitoba, on procedures for hand selecting wheat represented a small portion of the many public education forums organized by the Winter Fair board.

This fair was not at all like the summer show for with the exception of a few musical interludes, there was little in the way of entertainment. The winter fair was by and for the farmers. Many townsfolk came to watch the horse judging and view the various exhibits, but their interest was clearly of secondary importance. The fair directors justifiably took considerable pride in the farmers' attention to their show, for educating the agricultural community and honoring their accomplishments were the primary functions of the Brandon Winter Fair.

Although the livestock shows played an important role in both the summer and winter fairs, they had separate purposes. The summer competition was essentially a production show, with the farmers exhibiting and selling their breeding stock. The winter fair in contrast highlighted the finished product, the animals that were ready for market. This was a difference of critical importance to the agricultural exhibitors. The distinction was more than a technical one, for it governed the attitude of exhibitors and judges to the two contests.

The Brandon Winter Fair had established itself as Manitoba's premier livestock show and winter agricultural education event by 1912. In the spring of that year, following yet another successful fair, preparations were undertaken to expand the show once again. Acting Brandon Mayor Hughes and City Clerk H. Brown visited the provincial Legislature, requesting an amendment to the Brandon city charter which would permit the city to guarantee bonds issued by the winter fair for construction of a new building.

The provincial government agreed, allowing work to proceed on a $70,000 addition to the existing winter fair building.

Both the summer and winter fairs were clearly on their way by 1912. Brandon could and did boast of the most prestigious set of agricultural exhibitions in the Province of Manitoba. City promoters had long argued that their community was destined to be the agricultural cornerstone of the province, a claim that met firm resistance from the aggressive business and community leaders in Winnipeg. The proof though lay in the two fairs. The obvious farm interest in both shows, and the financial stability of both the winter and summer exhibitions pointed to broad public support for the promotion of agriculture. The city's claim to agricultural preeminence seemed unassailable and the agricultural exhibitions had led the way.

All signs hinted at an even rosier future. The Western Agricultural and Arts Association had great plans for the 1913 fair, slated to be a Dominion Exhibition, which they hoped would put their show on the national map. The Winter Fair board was completing arrangements for the construction of a handsome addition to their existing facility, hoping that the new space would allow for an expansion of exhibits and competitions, enabling the show to maintain its place at the forefront of the winter shows in western Canada. Both fairs had struggled to get to the top; the challenge now was staying there.

Chapter Two

1913 - 1929

Years of Growth

By 1912, THE SUMMER AND WINTER FAIRS had suffered through their growing pains and emerged as major partners in the western Canadian exhibition movement. As Brandon had grown, both in size and aspirations, so too had the fairs. These were exciting times, when the future prospects seemed unlimited and opportunity beckoned for all.

For Brandon and western Manitoba, the first years of the century's second decade were prosperous ones. The city was expanding rapidly, caught in the midst of a feverish building boom. New homes and businesses sprang up on every street as the burgeoning community spread out to the west and south.

The massive immigration flood which was first unleashed at the turn of the century peaked in 1912 and 1913. Tens of thousands of "New Canadians" boarded trains heading for the prairies, hoping to capitalize on the cheap farm land and the job prospects in the towns on the new frontier. Though other centres bore more of the brunt of this migration than did Brandon, it too became home to a rich ethnic mix in these halcyon years. Prosperity and growth were the call-words of the day, and both applied to Brandon and surrounding districts. With wheat prices high, and with a growing demand for livestock, the farmers and cattlemen of western Manitoba joined in the good times, and shared the common belief that the area would know an even more prosperous future.

For the summer fair, this period opened on a high note. The 1913 exhibition was more than just an expansion on the previous year's show, for in that year the city hosted the prestigious Dominion Exhibition. Each year, the federal government designated one of the country's larger fairs as the Dominion Exhibition and supported it with a $50,000 grant for buildings and prizes. There was much at stake in the on-going battle for Dominion Fair status, and the various exhibitions across the country competed vigorously for this honor.

The official designation, like so many federal honors, was distributed on a carefully chosen political basis, ensuring that all regions received their turn and that no major centre felt unduly slighted. There was more at stake than the money; to the victor went the legitimate claim of being the biggest and most important exhibition in the region. As well, the generous cash grant provided the winning fair association with the means to improve and expand its facilities.

For years, Brandon had fought for the right to host a Dominion Exhibition, though it was not until the establishment of the Western Manitoba Big Fair in 1897 that their appeals had much foundation. To their chagrin, if not their surprise, they lost out to Winnipeg. In 1904, the Winnipeg Industrial Exhibition hosted the Dominion Exhibition and used the federal funds to offer a lavish $100,000 in prizes, enough to threaten Brandon's claims to equal status.

But the Western Agricultural and Arts Association would not give up. They continued their appeals, hoping that the growth and importance of their annual summer show would sway the opinions of officials in the federal Department of Agriculture. It finally worked. After numerous submissions, often backed by personal representations, the federal government granted the coveted Dominion Exhibition designation to the Brandon fair for 1913. The official telegram was received on September 6th 1912. The *Brandon Sun* claimed:

> Probably no better time could have been chosen for the holding of the big gathering here. Next year Brandon will have its street car system in operation and the greater part of its other civic improvements completed. It is now up to the citizens of Brandon and more especially the different organizations in this city to get behind the fair association and make it one of the most successful events ever held in Western Canada.

The W.A.A.A. quickly laid plans to turn out the biggest show ever. The old grandstand was torn down, and replaced by a $40,000 structure which could seat 5,000. New display buildings were erected, the race track was replaced and the grounds and facilities otherwise expanded and improved. Eighty more acres of land

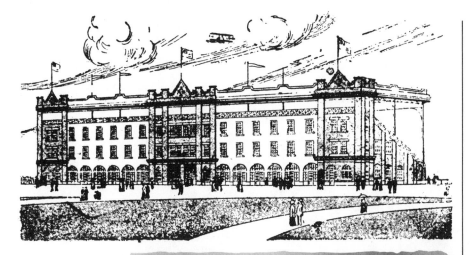

33　*The winter fair building, July 1913. Transportation in transition—people on foot, in buggys, in cars and on the new street cars. Brandon's first street cars began operating in June of 1913. One route went along 10th Street, turning west to 13th, then south to Exhibition Park. During fair week trailers were attached to the cars to help move the crowds. On one day during the Great War 14,000 passengers were transported to the fair grounds.*

34　*A sketch of the new grandstand.*

35　*A.C. McPhail, director and past-president. On 24 March 1908 he wrote Sir Clifford Sifton requesting his assistance to get the Dominion Exhibition for Brandon. McPhail's handwritten letter may be seen in the Public Archives of Canada, Ottawa. It concludes with the sentence, "…it would be appreciated if we could secure the Dominion Fair for one year and incidentally the grant of $50,000 which accompanies it."*

෴ *1913 17 July*
Directors of the Dominion Exhibition today announced "severe action", against shoe shine stores in Brandon. During the period of the fair the shoe-shiners raised their prices to 15 cents from 10 cents, and the exhibition board views this as gouging. The board decided to "install a small army of boot-blacks at various points throughout the city," to thwart the move, and have asked the police to take direct action.

36 *Cover of the 1913 Dominion Exhibition Prize List.*

37 *A six-horse hitch pulls the teamsters' entry in the Travellers' Day Parade, Dominion Exhibition, 1913.*

PRIZE LIST

DOMINION
EXHIBITION
BRANDON
MANITOBA
July 15th to 25th 1913

were purchased, bringing the fair grounds to a full 200 acres. Existing buildings, such as the Crystal Palace, were spruced up for this special show.

Buoyed by the federal grant, exhibition officials approached Brandon city council and neighboring municipalities for assistance. The majority of them graciously increased their previous grants to assist with this once-in-a-lifetime opportunity to put western Manitoba on display for the entire nation. Elton gave $700, while Cornwallis, Whitehead and Oakland gave $500 each, significant increases over their previous contributions. Other municipalities followed suit, supporting a show which for years had supported their farmers.

The councils were not the only ones to support this special event. A number of local, provincial and national companies pledged cash grants to add to the prize lists, allowing the exhibition to put together a record $21,000 for agricultural competitions and $20,000 for horse racing events. Collecting this money was not always easy. Early in 1913, the Brandon Hotelkeepers Association offered $3,000 for prizes for a Hotelkeeper's Stake. Preliminary discussions led to what the exhibition directors felt was a firm commitment to a $2,000 prize. Just a month before the event, the association informed the fair that the contribution had been reduced to only $1,000. Though the Hotel Association was reluctant to provide a full explanation, it was suggested that the failure of one of their members to win a major exhibition contract for his brickyard led to the withdrawal of part of the support. Fortunately most efforts to secure financial assistance went more smoothly.

THE BRANDON DOMINION EXHIBITION was officially opened on July 15th 1913, by Manitoba Premier Sir Rodmond Roblin before a crowd of over 15,000. It was a spectacular success from the very beginning. All agreed that from the agricultural competitions which attracted entries from across the country and the Travellers' Day Parade to the $5,000 fireworks finale, the Dominion fair was the best ever. Dozens of Canadian and American implement firms, drawn by the prospects of a huge farm audience, set up such a lively competition for prime exhibit space that the exhibition directors had to settle the conundrum by drawing names from a hat!

The fair was an overwhelming success, even though a later accounting revealed a sizable deficit. Although the announced gate attendance must be taken with a grain of salt, the claim that some 200,000 people bought tickets during the ten-day event provides some measure of the public's enthusiasm. The crush of humanity taxed the capacity of both the city and exhibition. Hotels were filled to capacity and exhibition directors once again appealed to the public for assistance in boarding the visitors. J. Granger and Sons found a more enterprising option. They rented the roller rink on the Winter Fair grounds and offered, for a fee, both meals and rudimentary sleeping accommodation. The scale of this operation is indicated by their claim that they could serve meals to 600 people at a time.

The farmers were not forgotten in the mad shuffle. The editor of the *Brandon Sun* complimented the exhibition association on its treatment of the fair's agricultural components:

> There is one thing which the directors have been ever ready to keep in mind and that is that Brandon's fair is first, last and all the time a farmers' fair. This year the holding of the Dominion Fair, despite the fact that more attention had to be directed to the many features which go to make up a national exhibition, has evidently brought no change of mind to those responsible for the arrangement of the fair. Each section has received attention, but the sections devoted to agricultural pursuits have been well cared for. The agricultural features have always been the leading features at Brandon, and as in the past so they are again this year.

ଚ *1913 25 July*

*"J.W. Marks, of 144
22nd Street, a lecturer at
Brandon College, narrowly
escaped with his life in a
bizarre incident at the
Dominion Exhibition. Marks
was one of a group of men
holding on to ropes which
kept a hot air balloon from
floating away. When the
order came to release their
hold, Marks could not, for the
rope was tangled around his
arm. He was carried aloft to
a height of 600-700 feet and
came to earth several blocks
away when the balloon made
its descent.   Two or three
women swooned during the
enactment of this dramatic
episode and the occurrence
will remain a lurid picture in
their memories until their
dying day."*
from the *Brandon Sun.*

ଚ *1913 30 July*

*Aviator W.H. Blakeley
today leaves Brandon to fly
to Boissevain to give exhibitions with his flying machine.
From there he will fly to
Virden for similar performances. Mr. Blakeley hopes he
may return to Manitoba next
summer with a machine large
enough to accommodate
passengers.*

38   *Midway, from the air,
Brandon fair.*

If the farmers were happy, so were the city-dwellers. A dazzling array of free shows, like the parachute drop and fireworks display, kept everyone entertained. An enlarged midway, halls filled with school exhibits and ladies' homecraft competitions, commercial displays and other features rounded out the exhibition package. There were few words of protest and many of praise as the special fair drew to a close.

Co-operation between the exhibition association and the city police ensured that the perpetual scourge of the exhibition circuit, the thieves and pickpockets, were kept at bay. A staff of detectives and plain-clothes officers, including several brought in from Winnipeg and the United States, patrolled the grounds under the supervision of Chief Berry. Loiterers were questioned, arrested or evicted from town. The local newspaper reported that:

> No less than twenty of the best known criminals on the continent came with the opening of the fair but ere long they safely landed in the jail to wait there until the big fair was over.

The work of the "slippery-fingered crew" had too often cast a pall over the fair-time proceedings, and the expeditious handling of this problem in 1913 earned well-deserved plaudits for those involved.

WITH THE DOMINION FAIR BEHIND THEM, the exhibition directors could confidently look to the future. Before the glow of the 1913 Exhibition had faded, however, they learned what the extravaganza had cost them. The large crowds and enthusiastic response to the giant undertaking made this a considerable surprise, but the directors nonetheless dipped into their pockets once again to provide guarantees and loans for the exhibition. Such petty financial concerns could, for a time, be ignored in the euphoria remaining from the Dominion Exhibition. For association directors, agricultural promoters and fair-goers in general, these were the best of times.

The genuine excitement evident in 1913 was not due solely to the anticipation surrounding the Dominion Exhibition. The Winter Fair generated its share of drama and civic pride too, ensuring that 1913 would indeed be a memorable year. The problems of the two previous years were over. The Brandon Mental Asylum fire, which caused the Winter Fair Pavilion to be occupied as temporary quarters for the patients, had forced the winter fair to schedule a reduced spring show, with the cattle shows held at the summer fair grounds and the poultry competitions situated in the Armory. The fair had pushed ahead, but less than perfect accommodations significantly reduced attendance and interest. Not so in 1913.

Plans had been in place for several years to build a major arena for the winter fair. The existing facilities, particularly the Pavilion, were too small to host the show. In 1911, the winter fair association borrowed $7,200 from its members to buy a block of land on the east side of 11th street, between Victoria and McTavish, which was reserved for the new building. Arranging plans and financing for the 5,000 seat arena proved rather more difficult.

In 1912, the association authorized the issuing of $70,000 worth of bonds and called for an architects' competition. After careful consideration of the plans submitted by four architects, the directors accepted, with slight modifications, the submission of Thomas Sinclair. By July 1912, tenders had been called and the preliminary construction contract of $52,000 was issued to Charles W. Hall. Preparations did not proceed as smoothly as anticipated. The steel work undertaken by Wisconsin Bridge and Iron Company came in some $900.00 over budget; there was a dispute with another supplier over the quality of the bricks; the directors had to issue more bonds to cover the escalating costs; and in December a rather nasty dispute arose with architect Sinclair over the project's progress. At the last meeting of 1912, a financial statement revealed that the building had already cost $71,000, with some $40,000 more needed to complete the building and finish paying for the land. Though some of the problems lingered, including the dispute with Sinclair (which resulted in the withholding of part of his wage), as the finishing touches were put on the elegant structure, the past disputes faded into insignificance.

It was an exuberant audience of over 4,500 which gathered on 3 March 1913 to celebrate the opening of the new facility. An impressive group of dignitaries, headlined by Manitoba Lieut. Governor D.C. Cameron, a former Brandon area resident, spoke eloquently and long—on the glories of the winter fair and the magnificent accomplishments of the Brandon Winter Fair Association. Most took time to highlight the important role of association president J.D. McGregor, who had spearheaded the project from the beginning.

THE NEW FACILITY provided an excellent site for the winter fair events. Thousands attended the ever-popular horse and livestock judging events. The success of local exhibitors was received with particular enthusiasm. J.D. McGregor's entry Glencarnock Boy beat all competitors to carry away top honors in its class. There was similar excitement during the special Clydesdale competition, won by another long-time Brandon farmer A.C. McPhail. In one of the main events, the selection of the Grand Champion Clydesdale, top prize went to R. Sinton's Gartly Bonus. His victory was loudly cheered:

> As soon as the eagerly waited decision was given by the judges the friends of the horseman in charge of Gartly Bonus rushed into the arena and carried him in triumph around the ring. R. Sinton, the proud owner, was then treated in a similar fashion, while the concourse of spectators rent the air with deafening cheers.

The cattle did not seem to share the enthusiasm for the new facility. The cheering crowds, the boisterous bands and the lively antics of the attendants created a festive ringside atmosphere, but one disturbing to the livestock. Some of the animals became excited when entering the arena, and their subsequent scrambles provided great amusement for the audience.

The 1913 winter fair was not an entertainment event. The emphasis was on agricultural competition and education, and little effort was expended on amusements. The lack of frivolity did not deter spectators. Dr. Bell, manager of the Winnipeg Exhibition, declared that "Brandon was the most horse-loving city that he knew, and the people of Brandon would do anything for a horse." He must have been right. Anticipating a larger than ever audience due to the new building, manager W.I. Smale ordered 20,000 tickets for the fair, which sold at $1.00 each. This was not enough, and by the middle of the fair Smale was borrowing tickets from the Summer Fair in order to meet the rush. In total, some 38,000 people attended the six-day event. The Brandon Winter Fair was a great success, and the new arena was the star attraction. (One "crank" obviously did not share that enthusiasm, for only a few months later, in July 1913, the Brandon fire department narrowly prevented a cleverly laid arson plot which threatened to gut the brand new building.)

The Brandon Winter Fair did not take second place to any winter fair in the country. Even the euphoria generated by the Dominion Exhibition could not dim the genuine accomplishments of the winter fair association.

1913 proved to be a year without equal. The opening of the new arena and hosting of the Dominion Exhibition together turned the national spotlight on the Brandon fair. The few minor problems encountered during the two shows did not mar the city's reputation as a major exhibition centre. Brandon's commitment to agricultural excellence, and the support of the surrounding districts for the efforts of the Western Agricultural and Arts

1916 2 November
    The winter fair directors unanimously voted to advise the minister of agriculture that the principal of the Manitoba Agricultural College in Winnipeg, Prof. Reynolds, was acting in a manner antagonistic to the Brandon winter fair. He repeatedly attempted to entice the livestock breeders to hold their annual meetings in Winnipeg. It was agreed that, "there has always been an element at work to centralize everything in Winnipeg, but so far they have not had much success."

39   *A close-up of midway attractions.*

Farming Made Easy
By Using our

Easy Farming Machinery

$44.00

All the latest Gas Engines for saving labour.

View of our e x h i b i t at Brandon Exhibition 1913.

1 to 60 h. p. Stationery and Portable Engines and 30 h. p. Traction Engines always in stock.

Make our office your h e a d q u a t e r s while in Brandon.

Have your mail addressed to 801 Pacific Ave., our care.

THE CANADIAN STOVER GASOLINE ENGINE CO., Ltd.   **Brandon, Manitoba**

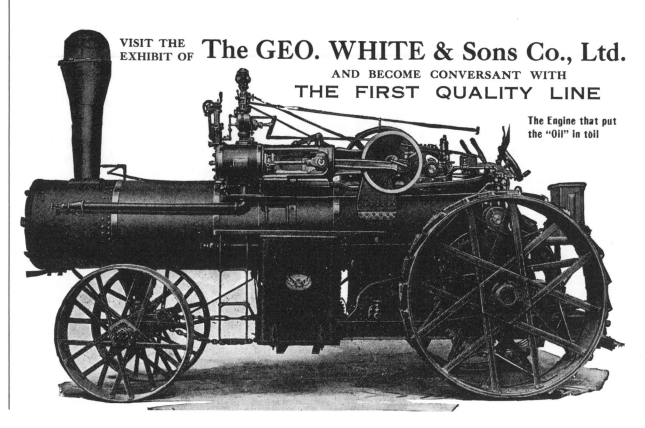

VISIT THE EXHIBIT OF **The GEO. WHITE & Sons Co., Ltd.**

AND BECOME CONVERSANT WITH
THE FIRST QUALITY LINE

The Engine that put the "Oil" in toil

40   *Advertisements from the 1913 and 1916 exhibition prize lists.*

58

Association and the Manitoba Winter Fair Association were clearly evident. Never before had Brandon's light shone quite so brightly.

Both events had one more run before the pall of war descended over the country. The winter fair of 1914 matched the previous year's show for quality and public support. The summer fair did not rise to quite the same heights, for obvious reasons, but the expanded facilities and enhanced reputation of the Inter-Provincial Exhibition ensured that the mid-summer event remained at the front rank of western Canadian fairs.

THE WAR YEARS WERE TO PROVIDE A SEVERE TEST of the fairs' durability. On 4 August 1914, Britain declared war on Germany. Almost immediately, Colonel Sam Hughes began the initial call-up of Canadian troops. Canada was at war, and the entire country seemed enveloped in mobilization and the excitement of war-time preparations. The resources of the nation were now at the beck and call of the government and the country geared up for a major contribution to the allied war effort.

The war would bring significant changes to the Canadian West. For the first three years, farmers and cattle breeders prospered. Urged on by the federal government, they patriotically expanded production, although they were also anxious to take advantage of the higher costs and insatiable demand for their products. Many were tempted into unwise expansion. They purchased more land, expanded onto marginal property, and bought more livestock and additional equipment. To finance this growth, numerous farmers borrowed, counting on a continuation

of prosperity to pay off their debts. But economic conditions soon deteriorated, and by war's end many farmers and cattlemen were in serious financial trouble. Prices fell, demand slackened, and the farmers of western Canada were left to pay massive bills in the midst of a falling market. The problems were largely of their own making, though the federal government's repeated appeals to patriotism and increased productivity had indubitably spurred them on.

The war brought other changes as well. The battles and sacrifices of the "Great War" challenged Canadians to improve their own society. If thousands of lives were being lost in a fight for democracy and liberty abroad, it seemed only just that further battles be waged against imperfections on the home front. Through the war years, such social causes as women's suffrage, prohibition, and urban reform found new supporters and, in several instances, success.

The war years provided an unusual setting for the frivolity and excitement of an exhibition. It seems rather incongruous to celebrate while thousands died on the battle field. The economic difficulties that farmers faced in the latter stages of the war further dampened enthusiasm and support for the summer and winter fairs. The new morality compounded the exhibitions' difficulties, as critics became even more insistent that "undesirable" elements be removed from the midway. Just to stage a fair in war-time was a major problem. Many fairs across the country closed their doors during the war years, patriotically declaring that all the country's resources had to be mobilized for military purposes.

Not all the exhibitions accepted this reasoning. The central purpose of the fair was to promote agricultural productivity and innovation. Now, more than ever, it was imperative to assist the farmers with their work. The exhibitions which followed this line believed they had to continue, if not expand, their work during the war. They too were making an important contribution to the war effort and to the reconstruction which would inevitably follow the end of hostilities. Although few made the point publicly, the summer fairs also provided a unique opportunity to escape the horrors of war, at least for a time.

The war years proved to be a difficult time for Western Canadian fairs. Many turned over their facilities to the armed forces for use as mobilization or training centres. Others, like the Vancouver exhibition, pushed on, though the decision to proceed generated some genuine anger toward the fair. The Winnipeg Exhibition collapsed during the war. Although attendance remained high in 1914, constant financial losses and less than enthusiastic support from city fathers resulted in the cancellation of the 1915 exhibition. It would be years before a serious attempt was made to resurrect the Winnipeg fair.

The Western Agricultural and Arts Association struck a middle ground between these extremes. The fair continued, but a special accommodation was reached with the Canadian army. As well, efforts were made to bring the exhibition into line with the new demands for moral purity and the striving for a "Brave New Canada."

The exhibition association was anxious to do its share for the war effort. Though the proposal faced considerable internal opposition, the W.A.A.A. agreed in November 1914 to turn over the fair grounds free of charge to the government for use as a prisoner-of-war camp. The only provision was that the grounds be released in time for the annual show. That offer was not accepted, but when Colonel McRae, Chief Remount Officer, requested the use of the facilities as a Central Mobilization Station, the directors willingly complied. The grounds were so used throughout the war, though arrangements were made so that the fair could proceed. Considerable damage resulted from the occupation, but the government provided full compensation at war's end.

ɛ❧ *1920 29 March*
"The largest cheque for prize winnings ever paid out at a Brandon Summer or Winter Fair was issued from the Winter Fair offices today by Secretary Smale to James Turner of Carroll. The cheque amounted to $1,040, the previous high figure being $740. This cheque does not include the prize money won by Mr. Turner's son in the Calf and Continuation classes. Mr. Smale stated today that as far as he was aware, the cheque for $1,040 handed to Mr. Turner is the largest cheque of its kind ever issued from an exhibition or fair in Canada. The money is solely for prizes actually won in competition at the Winter Fair by cattle from Mr. Turner's farm. The total prize money issued from the fair office for the Winter Fair is about $14,000."
from the *Brandon Sun*.

41   *A military parade on Rosser Avenue.*

🍀 1920 22 July

"DAREDEVIL CAMPBELL FLIRTS WITH DEATH; SENSATION OF FAIR. Mark Campbell Stands With Outstretched Arms On Top of Swiftly Moving Plane, Over Which He Later Crawls Like a Human Fly—Hangs by Legs From Gear Beneath Plane While Travelling More Than Fifty Miles an Hour— Rounded Roof of Plane Driven by Casewell Bears Nothing That Affords a Safe Handhold Even When Resting on the Ground." headlines from the *Brandon Sun.*

42   *Katherin Stinson was a famous aviatrix from the period of the First World War. In 1915 she flew her bi-plane to Brandon and landed it at Exhibition Park. This advertisement is from the 1916 Exhibition prize list.*

This is One of the Attractions that You Will See at the Provincial Exhibition

MISS KATHERIN STINSON
Tangoes in the Sky with a Speedy Biplane

Miss Stinson is the ONLY Woman in the world who ever looped the loop, day and night, with and without fireworks.

The war caused other problems for the summer show. The heavy demand on transportation facilities resulted in severe restrictions on the shipment of carnival attractions and livestock exhibits. Negotiations with the federal government and the railway companies resulted in some modifications of transportation arrangements, although higher prices and long waits for access to the main line slowed the shipment of fair-related material.

The exhibition association had trouble protesting such regulations too vociferously, for to do so smacked of self-interest and a lack of patriotic spirit. To the contrary, the fair management did their utmost to demonstrate their support for Canada's war effort. Soldiers were allowed on the grounds at reduced prices, special veterans' tents were erected, and military equipment was brought to the fair as a special attraction.

War-time limitations also encouraged the Brandon fair to become more active in the Western Canada Fair Association. The demise of the Winnipeg show had seriously hampered the ability of the western Manitoba fair to attract suitable carnival and attraction companies, and so the association turned to the broader network. In 1918, the fair circuit contracted with Johnny J. Jones for the carnival and Mayerhoff Attractions of New York for the "platform" performers. In this instance, the association forced the Brandon fair to shift its dates to accommodate the other exhibitions, a risky move made necessary by the demands of the circuit.

The Brandon summer show carried on with much the same attractions and carnivals as before. Auto racing was added to the program for the first time and proved very popular with fair-goers. The federal government's encouragement of farm mechanization and the manufacturing companies' desire to place their products in front of the farmers ensured a large annual display of tractors and other equipment. The presentation was further amended to incorporate a tractor-plowing demonstration on land rented for the project.

62

43   *Winning six-horse teams line up for a parade in front of the grandstand, c.1915.*

44   *A typical farm scene, Gladstone, Manitoba, 1916, well before hydro, well before technology.*

45   *For many years the Women's Hospital Aid operated a dining room at the summer fair. This picture, taken in 1915 or 1916, shows organizers and volunteer waitresses in front of the building. Centre front is Mrs. Thomas Lee, and behind her Mrs. A.B. Weir. The waitresses include Effie Weir, Alma Stinson, and Ann Galbraith.*

AUTO RACES

BRANDON EXHIBITION
FRIDAY ONLY, JULY 26TH

"WILD" BILL ENDICOTT

Veteran driver and winner of many speed battles.

SIG. HAUGDAHL

Only Scandinavian driver campaigning the American dirt tracks.

JULES ELLINGBUE

Holder of Canadian National Championship and world's two-mile record.

7 Long and Short Distance Races. **7**

$3,000 IN PRIZES AND BONUSES

Top—JULES ELLINGBUE

Bottom—LEON DURAY

"WILD" BILL ENDICOTT

LEON DURAY

Daring French driver.

LARRY DOYLE

CLIFFORD TOFT
Pacific Coast star.

BOB CLINE

Youngest driver of high powered cars in America. And others.

Races Sanctioned, and all Drivers Licensed, by International Motor Contest Association.

ENTERED IN BRANDON RACES LAST DAY OF EXHIBITION, FRIDAY, JULY 26TH

Mr. Farmer:

Why send your money to the United States or to Eastern Canada when you can do better right here in Brandon on anything you need in the way of Gasoline Engines, Windmills, Feed Grinders, Roller Crushers, Iron and Wood Pumps, Pumping Jacks, Steel or Wood Saw Frames, etc.

We can give you as good service and as close prices as any concern in Canada. Buy Western Canada-made goods and help build up manufacturing plants in your own country. This will help to increase the value of your lands and furnish a market for your products.

Our full line will be on exhibit. Call and see us.

Manitoba Engines Limited

BRANDON, Man.   and   CALGARY, Alta.

46 *Automobile racing was a new and exciting attraction in the twenties. Ad from the Brandon Sun.*

47 *An early nationalistic pitch, from the 1916 exhibition program.*

❧ *1921 22 January*
Mr. N.W. Kerr com-plained that there was an "information leak" on the board. Someone had advised Mr. Kerr's law partner, G.B. Coldwell, that Mr. Kerr had opposed the purchase of a block of property that Mr. Coldwell offered to sell to the exhibition board.

❧ *1921 22 July*
A prize of $35 has been offered for the best entry in the exhibition's bread-making competition. The prize list states that an entry consists of two loaves each weighing two pounds.

48   *W. Dowling, summer fair director and past-president, a pioneer Brandon merchant.*

THE GROWING CONCERN WITH MORAL PURITY and a desire for social reform placed new limits on what the exhibition could offer in its summer show. Opposition to the "girlie" shows and the games of chance increased, placing the association in a rather embarrassing situation. The main battle centered around race track betting. Before the war, the W.A.A.A. had been pressured by other western fairs to adopt para-mutuel betting machines, and eliminate the heavily criticized method of allowing one man to "book" the races, a system open to abuse. The exhibition agreed to adopt the system in 1914, but the plan came under attack during the war. Pressure from within and without the organization challenged the legitimacy of this prime attraction. Moral purity groups across western Canada petitioned the fairs to eliminate gambling.

As early as 1913, J.D. McGregor was suggesting that the horse races be eliminated and replaced with stock parades. That proposal received little support, but the issue did not die. A number of exhibition directors banded together to change the W.A.A.A. policy. A 1916 motion to eliminate betting from the fair schedule suffered a narrow defeat when President R.M. Matheson broke a tie vote by deciding in favour of betting. The protest movement soon broadened. Initial anger was directed at gambling; now the target seemed to be the races themselves. Hoping to forestall local and national protests, Mr. Dowling, chairman of the Speed Committee, convinced the fair board in 1917 to discontinue gambling, but proceed with a full card of horse events. The fair board rather liked having both racing and gambling on the grounds, but the ability of social reformers to link their demands for moral improvement with the imperatives of the national war effort made it extremely difficult for the association to resist the change. Gambling would return after the war, but for a time the purists had their way.

Despite the problems created by the war, the directors of the Western Agricultural and Arts Association did not lose sight of their larger ambitions for western Manitoba's fair. The collapse of the Winnipeg exhibition caused some immediate problems, making it more difficult to attract livestock exhibitors for example, but it also opened up some exciting opportunities. Brandon became Manitoba's only full-size summer exhibition and could thus seek the formal recognition which this implied. As manager W.I. Smale noted in 1916, "This is the time and this is the year for a progressive and aggressive policy. Good as our Exhibition is we can make it much better."

There was also considerable debate as to the best name for the summer show. With Winnipeg out of the way, the designation "Provincial Exhibition" seemed appropriate and was informally adopted by the middle of the war. For the time being, the majority supported retaining the old name, the "Inter-Provincial Fair." The question of a name would receive greater attention in a few years time. The main objective was securing the financial support and status due the province's most important agricultural show.

In view of this new status, the association decided to pursue greater provincial representation on the grounds and in the board room. A request was submitted for a special provincial building, which would provide a major display of the resource potential and human achievements of the province. There was also a concerted effort to broaden the association's base of public support. If the fair was to be a truly provincial show, it would have to call on representatives from throughout the province. Though formal constitutional changes would wait until after the war, the numerous vacancies on the board caused by death or departure from western Manitoba provided the impetus for a full-scale recruitment drive. An effort was underway to solidify the Brandon summer fair's claim to provincial pre-eminence.

The war years had not, finally, been that hard on the summer fair. Attendance and entries remained high, and with the modest

49 *Manitoba farm production on display at Los Angeles, 1915.*

50 *A poster used to promote Manitoba agricultural products at the Toronto fair, 1916.*

67

exception of complaints over racing, there were few complaints about the exhibition program. The demise of the Winnipeg fair had created a huge opening for the Brandon show, one the directors had every intention of exploiting. In addition, the expansion of the Western Canada fair circuit enhanced the ability of the individual fairs to recruit carnivals and other attractions. World War I had been a traumatic time for Canada, and the economic and social trials were felt particularly strongly in the West. The exhibition had served as a welcome oasis in the midst of the shortages, sacrifices and dislocations of war. The Western Agricultural and Arts Association emerged from the war years stronger than when the battles began.

THE SAME COULD NOT BE SAID for the winter fair. The Manitoba Winter Fair and Fat Stock Show association was called on to make a rather more substantial sacrifice for the war effort than was its summer counterpart. When the federal government was seeking troop accommodations in Brandon, the winter fair buildings were a natural choice. With a minimum of negotiation, the association agreed in November 1914 to lease the facilities for $600.00 per month. Unlike the W.A.A.A., the winter fair association was unable to secure a release of the buildings for the week of the fair.

There was little choice but to cancel the show for 1915 and 1916. It was initially hoped to shift the show to the summer fair grounds, but since the facility was being used for the mobilization of horses, that option was closed. The association was not, however, prepared to sacrifice its Boys' Fat Calf Class. Secretary W.I. Smale later wrote of this competition:

> Its primary object is to encourage the raising of good beef stock, but it serves another purpose, perhaps a more primary one, and that is that it educates and interests the rising generation in the livestock industry. No boy who receives the honor and admiration that a prize winner in this competition receives can fail to have a lasting impression made on his mind of the profitable and honorable side of the agricultural and livestock industry.

Not even the trauma of war prevented the directors from proceeding with this vitally important program. A $1,000 grant from Brandon banks provided the necessary funds to hold a small competition in a corner of the winter fair grounds.

The winter fair buildings did not sit idle. Soon after the government took over the facilities, they were turned into a detention centre for Ukrainian internees and other "enemy aliens." As many as 800 to 1,000 internees, Canadian residents and not prisoners of war, were locked up on the grounds. The Ukrainians did not take their detention without protest. In June 1915, an escape attempt of 17 Ukrainians ended with the tragic death of an 18-year-old, shot while trying to flee through a stable window. The drastic response deterred further such endeavors. By 1916, the demands of Canadian businesses and farmers for additional labor led to the gradual release of the internees, and within the year the winter fair buildings were emptied.

In 1917, the winter fair was back on schedule, although labor shortages and farmers' preoccupation with war-time production limited the number of entries and spectators. This show and the following one were modest successes, but did not produce enough money to retire the association's growing debt. Both the Brandon Winter Fair and Livestock Association, which managed the buildings for the provincial government, and the Manitoba Winter Fair and Fat Stock Association, the group responsible for the actual show, were experiencing financial problems. Their distress, coupled with the prosperity of the summer fair, led to a growing number of suggestions that the two bodies join in a common organization dedicated to the promotion of agriculture. The two associations had been working closely together since the inception of the winter fair. The provincial government indicated in 1918 that they were interested in supporting a joint association and encouraged the two fair associations to reach a suitable arrangement. Several meetings were held, culminating in joint resolutions by the winter fair and W.A.A.A. to consider formal amalgamation.

THE PROVINCIAL EXHIBITION

BRANDON, MANITOBA

JULY 1919

EVERY PROGRESSIVE FARMER AND BREEDER AND EVERY PROGRESSIVE CITIZEN SHOULD COMMENCE RIGHT NOW TO PREPARE FOR THE BIGGEST AND BEST EXHIBITION YET HELD IN BRANDON.

Let it be "Celebration" Week
A "Victory" Week For You

ATTRACTIVE PREMIUMS WILL BE OFFERED FOR EVERY BREED OF

Live Stock and Poultry,

Dairy Products,   Vegetables,   Horticulture

Fine Arts and Ladies' Work

ATTRACTIONS

WILL BE THE BEST EVER SEEN AT BRANDON'S BIG FAIR.

Make it Your Holiday Week.   It will pay you to do so

W. DOWLING, President.   W. I. SMALE, Secretary.

1922 28 July

"Chief elephant trainer Capt. Jack Davis of Johnny J. Jones Exposition, looking at his pets yesterday, decided after a practical glance over the pachyderm guests of the Brandon Fair that the toenails were too long. "Looks like it's high time we did a little manicuring around here," he muttered musingly, whereupon he called his assistant, Eddie West, to him and began preparations to reduce the cuticle growths of Gyp, Alice, and Baby Sue to the proper dimensions.

The manicure equipment which they brought forth and laid on the gravel did not resemble the tools which are to be seen on the small table in front of the marcelled operator in high class barber shops. There were no delicate scissors, rose sticks or bowls of perfumed water. Instead instruments consisted of a

continued

51 *Advertisement for the provincial exhibition from the 1919 winter fair prize list.*

couple of common building bricks, a wood file, a cake of yellow soap, something that looked like gasoline, and a pot of linseed oil.

"The elephants, who up to this time had been engaged in swinging their trunks to and fro, took a look at the preparations and then watched Capt. Davis as he approached. It was plain that the pachyderms were not enthusiastic about the toilet arrangements. "Come on Gyp, get along Alice, smile up Sue." Thereupon the elephants declared war. They lifted their trunks and emitted a noise that sounded like the blast of a toy trumpet. Persuasion was in vain. Even prods with the goad failed to affect them. "So you won't move, eh?" asked Mr. Davis. The trio indicated that they would not. "You've made up your minds?" The trio evidently had. "And nothing will induce you to give in to the manicuring?" The three beasts indicated that the Andes mountains would get up and walk before they would. "Very well, we'll see

52 *The Brandon business district, 1919.*

53 *Crowds throng the midway, c.1920.*

70

The effort had broad implications. J.D. McGregor informed the groups that Winnipeg was considering establishing both summer and winter fairs. If Brandon wanted to protect its position, it would have to act quickly. By moving when the Winnipeg movement was stalled, McGregor argued, they could secure official "Provincial" designation for both the winter and summer shows.

Matters seemed to be moving rapidly toward a satisfactory conclusion. Both the provincial and city governments favored the move, for it would make it easier to arrange grants and place the Brandon fairs on a more satisfactory footing. Both the Western Agricultural and Arts Association and the Manitoba Winter Fair Association passed separate resolutions favoring the amalgamation; several delegations met with Brandon city council and provincial representatives to discuss the matter, but it all came to naught.

In early April 1920, W.A.A.A. president William Downing and representatives R.M. Matheson, D.W. Agnew and W.I. Smale travelled with Kenneth Campbell of the Brandon Winter Fair and Livestock Association, Mayor Dinsdale, Alderman Curran and Alderman Hall to meet with the provincial cabinet. It seemed, at first, that agreement had been reached on the sale of the winter fair buildings to the summer fair association. The plan would have left the W.A.A.A. as the sole exhibition property owner in the city, with the Manitoba Winter Fair and Fat Stock Association becoming their tenants. This latter group opposed the idea, and told provincial politicians so during the 1920 Winter Fair. The opposition seemed to rest on the winter fair association's belief that their show would lose out under the union. Their request that the proposed agreement be withdrawn was accepted.

It was a bitter loss for the Western Agricultural and Arts Association, who felt that their ambitions of becoming a full "Provincial" exhibition were now dashed. The associations' representatives asked that the failure of negotiations not be allowed to interrupt their other plans. The politicians agreed, and on 3 April 1920, the Western Agricultural and Arts Association was

formally incorporated as the Provincial Exhibition of Manitoba, with all the status and financial assistance that this designation conveyed.

THE SUCCESS IN THE DECADES-OLD BATTLE for provincial status was seen in Brandon as only fitting. It was an unfamiliar victory over the capital city, so Brandonites could be forgiven if they crowed a little. A *Brandon Sun* editorial in 1921 reflected the chauvinism of western Manitoba exhibition boosters:

> Winnipeg has failed to establish an exhibition; Brandon has succeeded. Brandon has by long years of toil built up a successful exhibition; Winnipeg could not. Brandon has one of the finest sites in the west for an annual exhibition; Winnipeg has not. Brandon has a smooth working machinery for the production of a great exhibition; Winnipeg has proved itself incapable of constructing one....The co-operation of Winnipeg would help the province, its people, their business, provincial industries, the welfare of both communities and every district, if it were directed to a great effort to boost the Brandon exhibition. It has received little encouragement in its efforts from the first city of Manitoba, perhaps from jealousy.

It was not often Brandon won out over Winnipeg, and the city was determined to savor its victory.

The directors of the newly named Provincial Exhibition of Manitoba were anxious to make theirs a truly province-wide organization. Immediate consideration was given to expanding the size of the directorate to accommodate additional regional representatives. J.D. McGregor, president of the P.E.M., stated that "We should have the Provincial Fair in everything as well as name" and convinced the board to expand its membership to 20. W.W. Fraser, the provincial live stock commissioner, supported McGregor's assessment, saying that expanding the directorate would make the Provincial Exhibition "more provincial in its character, and in that way increasing its scope and usefulness."

A serious effort was made to raise the provincial profile of the western Manitoba show and disprove the belief that all provincial institutions had to be located in Winnipeg. The rivalry remained evident, and many P.E.M. directors retained their fear that a resurrection of the Winnipeg exhibition would inevitably lead to a decline in the status of the Brandon show. Others welcomed the prospect of another major Manitoba show, confident that their fair would remain pre-eminent and that together the two exhibitions could attract more entries and better attractions. During a November 1923 meeting held to discuss possible assistance to a proposed Winnipeg fair, director Fred Hobson captured the divided sentiments on the matter: "We are informed that the citizens of Winnipeg are reaching out to strangle our fair by an opposition fair in their city, but I do not believe anything of the kind, and am of the opinion that a fair in Winnipeg would be mutually beneficial." For most, the provincial designation and the continuing success of their summer program provided sufficient evidence of a profitable future.

There were other important signs of change. W.I. Smale, secretary-manager of both the summer and winter fairs since 1910, quit. Smale had provided dedicated and professional service for many years. During the war, he had twice turned down salary increases; in 1916, he asked for a bonus of $100 instead of an additional $500 in salary. The following year, he accepted a part-time position as treasurer of the Livestock Breeders' Association, but turned his $1,000 salary back to the W.A.A.A. and used it to hire additional office help.

Smale's last year at the exhibition proved to be rather stormy. Through the years, he had been given considerable freedom in handling the daily administrative and planning duties of the association, tasks which all members agreed he handled exceptionally well. In 1923, the directors began both to question and

outfitted the new arrivals with horses for their draught power and livestock for their sustenance.

He soon acquired a small parcel of property north and west of Brandon where he began a farming operation. Eventually he added adjoining properties and developed them as "Gwenmawr" which became a showplace on the eastern prairies. Here he began the Glencarnock line of Aberdeen Angus cattle on which was built his reputation as a breeder of championship stock.

"J.D." had an unerring knack for recognizing power. He developed a close affiliation with a young Brandon lawyer named Clifford Sifton and this association continued for years. Sifton wanted to be elected to Parliament, and he chose "J.D." as his campaign manager. This successful partnership, forged in frontier friendship, grew in importance as Sifton, later Sir Clifford, trusted his ally with responsibilities both delicate and demanding. With a business base firmly established in Brandon, and with Sifton's success in Ottawa, McGregor was able to become active in areas far distant from the valley of the Assiniboine. He served in the Yukon as Sifton's inspector of mines and later became commissioner of liquor licences in the same territory. (When he left the

continued

73

Yukon, he made certain that his lucrative positions were filled by someone friendly to him, and he arranged to be succeeded by his brother Colin.) Fascinated with projects of heroic proportions, he established a ranch of 200,000 acres in Alberta on which he maintained a herd of 15,000 range cattle.

Journalists of the time, and historians of a later period, insisted that these undertakings were possible only because of political favoritism. There can be no denying that patronage was involved. In the Alberta land transactions, McGregor paid only a peppercorn leasehold rent of five cents an acre for land he eventually bought for $1 an acre and sold for many times that figure, and he was managing director of another extensive holding which he sold to British investors as the South Alberta Cattle Company. His nature was such, however, that he easily shrugged off charges that all of his success was possible only because he was a confidante of a powerful minister of government.

But, no matter where he might be temporarily located on assignment for Sir Clifford Sifton, McGregor never neglected his duties at Gwenmawr. His success with his Glencarnock herd was such that in 1912 he captured the grand championship at the Chicago International Live-

repudiate his actions. Smale had arranged for the shipment of certain supplies to Brandon at prices association members deemed excessive. Smale handed in his resignation at the same meeting, citing ill health as the reason for his departure, though that did not stop the directors from deducting 50% of the transportation costs from the former manager's salary. It was later shown that Smale had made several promises regarding prize lists and competitions that the board had not authorized. Again, this had been standard procedure in the past, but the association gave notice that the promises made were not to be considered binding.

It seemed that an illustrious career was coming to an inglorious end. A.J. Hacher was hired as a short-term replacement while a search was begun for a permanent manager. The directors soon retracted most of their actions against Smale. At the November annual meeting, the board members passed a motion expressing "their deep appreciation of his services, the giving of his time and talent without stint or consideration of his health." They also retracted their earlier demands that Smale repay outstanding transportation costs. Smale continued in ill health, and died on 3 October 1924.

THE SUMMER FAIR BOARD had already completed its search for a replacement. Hacher worked through the summer of 1923, and on 13 September 1923 the board decided to hire J.E. Rettie, former manager of the Ontario provincial winter fair at Guelph, who received an annual salary of $3,600. Although Rettie was hired to manage both the summer and winter shows, it appears as though the selection and negotiations were conducted solely by the Provincial Exhibition of Manitoba. The Manitoba Winter Fair did, however, contribute to his salary. Rettie was able to build on the solid legacy left from his predecessor, and, over the next decade and a half, put his own imprint on the Brandon exhibitions.

One of Rettie's major pre-occupations was the encouragement of the western Canadian fair circuit. Over the previous decade, fair associations in the west had recognized the importance of working together. The process began in a modest fashion, with several exhibitions joining together to hire a single carnival company or arranging fair dates to enable exhibitors to show in a series of fairs. This arrangement was formalized in 1915 when the Western Canada Fair and Racing Circuit and Western Canada Fair Managers' Association merged to become the Western Canada Fair Circuit.

Accepting membership in the summer fair circuit put some rather stringent restrictions on the actions of the Brandon fair. In 1923, the selection of dates brought the Provincial Exhibition into direct conflict with the smaller Manitoba fairs. The directors decided to stick with the July dates. As one member noted "We must stay in the circuit in which we are at present; to withdraw means suicide, and cannot for a moment be even contemplated." The issue was not an easy one, for many directors wanted the Brandon fair to remain as the "clearing house" for Manitoba's small exhibitions. In the end, the decision was made to stick with the Class "A" circuit. Rather quickly, the smaller fairs realized the need to have a major fair in their area, and they too came to accept Brandon's decision.

The circuit debate flared again in 1928. Regina demanded a change of dates which, if accepted, would have forced the Brandon exhibition to accept an even earlier schedule. To most directors this was unacceptable. A committee headed by manager Rettie was appointed to examine the question of circuits and to look in particular at the possibility of joining the North Dakota Fair Circuit. Although it seemed at first that the North Dakota association offered as much as the Western Canadian Fair Circuit, the committee soon discovered that the move would carry significant costs. The Provincial Exhibition directors noted with smug satisfaction that their fair was superior to those south of the line,

stock show with Glencarnock Victor; the year following he repeated the feat with Glencarnock Victor II. This strain dominated his herd until 1920 when he acquired Black Cap Revolution, another herd sire of international reputation which he eventually sold for $15,000.

The "Laird of Glencarnock" was a leader and an innovator. He is credited with introducing alfalfa into the West, and he led in the practice of using sweet clover and field corn as fodder. No aspect of husbandry escaped his attention; at one time he operated 800 colonies of bees, which made him the province's major producer of honey.

In many of his early speeches to farm associations, McGregor displayed a willingness to take the initiative once he had determined a course of action. He was among the first farmers to pressure the provincial government to begin a system of agricultural representatives, professionally-trained agrologists to communicate the latest farm information to the producers.
He had a passion for organization. He wanted Ottawa to establish a national goal for agriculture, to meet changing market conditions. He was an advocate of "local agricultural committees," semi-formal associations that could be used to spread the

continued

and that Brandon would be best served by staying with the large urban exhibitions in western Canada. Regina was, in this instance, convinced to back down although this was not to be the last conflict over dates.

The exhibition association also found money to improve the fair grounds. The effort was considerably more modest than the pre-World War I period, largely because so many new buildings and general improvements had been made for the 1913 Dominion Exhibition. In 1920, for example, work proceeded on an Administration Building, but a larger plan for a new display building had to be scrapped due to lack of money.

THE FIRST MAJOR PROJECT IN THE 1920s was a new provincial building. After securing the official "Provincial" designation in 1920, the association repeatedly petitioned the Manitoba government to establish a more formal presence during the summer show. For many years, various government departments had hosted exhibits during the fair, but little was done to tie the provincial administration's contribution together. It made sense to erect a separate building, and to put the province on display.

A suitable arrangement was reached in 1926. The exhibition association would proceed with a $25,000 exhibit building which the province agreed to lease on a ten-year basis to pay off the costs of construction. It was appropriately named the Manitoba Government Building. When Premier John Bracken officially opened the facility on 4 July 1927, he enthusiastically remarked, "No expenditure has ever been made so gladly by the government, than the expense put into this new building." In that first year, the Departments of Forestry, Mines, and Game, as well as the Labor Bureau, the Fire Protection Branch, the Manitoba Agricultural College, the Bureau of Health Nurses, the Manitoba School for the Deaf, the Brandon Mental Hospital and representatives from the provincial government's Dairy, Livestock, and Poultry

è❧ *1924 3 March*

Two groups of farm women, the United Farm Women's chapters of Forrest, and Little Souris, petitioned the fair board to protect young boys from the evils of liquor while at the fair. "The secretary is instructed to write these ladies informing them that the police would be asked to take particular care in noting whether such a practice was taking place, and if so, to do all in their power to have the same stopped."
from the minutes

54 *Manitoba Government Building.*

55 *Advertisement in the 1919 winter fair prize list.*

branches of the Department of Agriculture all hosted displays. In addition, the new building was the site for the Women's Institute exhibit, the Boys' and Girls' Club competitions, an exhibit of first aid treatment, and displays from the public schools.

The Manitoba Government Building was not the only major construction project in the decade. Through the early 1920s, automobiles played an increasingly important part in the exhibition. The general improvement in the quality of roads and the increasing number of people owning automobiles brought this industry front and centre on the exhibition grounds. As early as 1919, exhibition manager W.I. Smale remarked on the impact of automobiles on the fair:

> The automobile has had a great deal to do with increasing the gate receipts, for it seems that everyone within a radius of fifty miles who has a car or whose friends or acquaintances have a car comes to the fair via auto. In the last year or two it has become a problem to accommodate all the autos which come, for the grounds are far too small and the space is too much in demand for other purposes to accommodate more than six or eight hundred autos.

Local automobile dealers recognized the exciting commercial prospects of displaying at the fair, and approached the association in 1926 for permission to build a separate automobile building. The proposal was not immediately accepted, and the car dealers had to be content with the rather cramped quarters assigned to them under the grandstand. When the dealers suggested they might consider holding a show at the Winter Fair building during the summer fair, the association began to look on their request for a separate building more favorably.

The Provincial Exhibition Association decided to proceed with the construction of an Automobile Building, borrowing $6,500 at below market rates from Peter Payne and N.W. Kerr to pay for the project. Even before this, seven Brandon automobile dealers, McCreary's Limited, Lehigh Motors, Western Motors, Thomas J.

Clark, Canadian Motors Ltd., Brydson and Lyons, and F.M. Stephens, had agreed to rent space for a three-year period, guaranteeing full occupation of the building before it was even built.

The Automobile Building became a major fair attraction when it opened for the first time in 1927. Those dealers who had not moved quickly enough to gain display space now petitioned the association for an addition. There was not enough money to proceed in 1928, but private loans were secured the following year which allowed construction to commence on a 60′ x 100′ addition to the main structure. This too was fully subscribed even before it opened. The enlarged Automobile Building drew large and enthusiastic crowds, and the dealers reported numerous sales to the fair-goers. The whole episode offers another example of the commercial value of the summer show and the appreciation of local businesses for the marketing opportunities provided by the summer spectacular.

THE PROVINCIAL EXHIBITION had lost none of its appeal or drawing power through the war years; and in the 1920s quickly re-asserted its place in the hearts of urban and rural fair-goers alike. A news reporter for the *Brandon Sun* captured the mystifying attraction of the fair-time pot-pourri:

> Where would we toilworn mortals be without the jovial, tinselled, jazzy midway? What is it when even the stagiest old stager enters the fair grounds, that makes him hold his head a little higher, prick up his ears and quicken his pace? Nothing more than the burst of harmonious discordancy that breaks upon his ears from the midway. When he can hear the sound of the hoarse voice of the perspiring showman roaring through his megaphone, the weird howls of the wild man, the clash of the cymbals, the deep rub-a-dub-dub of the drum, the triumphant strains of the merry-go-round, the shouts of the lemonade seller, the earnest exhortations of the hot dog man, the impassioned appeals of the artist with the

56 *N.W. Kerr, summer fair director and past-president. In company with director Peter Payne he loaned the exhibition board money for the new building.*

balloons and whips, the seductive tones of the lady with four rings for a dime—when he hears all these things, he becomes young again, and promises himself a couple of hours on the midway.

It was quite a show, true to the management's claims that there was something for everyone. The 1921 summer fair which drew an estimated audience of 100,000 reflected the continued success of the summer show. Great emphasis was placed on the agricultural components. Over 2,000 head of livestock were on display, filling the barns to capacity. The horse show drew a full complement of exhibitors, and light horse competitions, despite the increasing popularity of the "Tin Lizzies," remained a crowd favorite. An aviary exhibit, a butter and egg show, an impressive horticultural exhibit and a poultry competition demonstrated the commitment of the Provincial Exhibition of Manitoba to the promotion of agriculture.

The exhibition association, having long since learned that agricultural exhibits did not bring in the crowds, made efforts to highlight the stock parades and to emphasize the competitions in a few of the "glamour" classes, like heavy horses. The principal emphasis however lay with education and entertainment. A series of displays in the Dominion building and the Crystal Palace informed fair-goers of the work of their federal and provincial governments while offering advice on agricultural, economic and domestic affairs. A handsome display of the best work produced by school children of western Manitoba, in penmanship, woodworking and art, demonstrated the accomplishments of the province's school system. Special presentations from the Department of Indian Affairs' residential schools demonstrated the "progress" of native children.

Children had a high profile at the 1921 summer exhibition. Boys and Girls clubs had been established during the First World War, but assumed even greater prominence after 1918. In 1921, a series of boys' teams from around western Manitoba competed in livestock judging. For the girls, the competitions focused on the emerging science of "home economics." The displays illustrated the range of instruction received through the clubs:

A girls team from Elva will demonstrate textiles—the different uses and kinds of goods, matching and other phases of textile work. Artistic home decoration will be displayed by a girls team from Medora who will completely dismantle a poorly furnished and decorated room and redecorate it. Transforming wheat into bread will be demonstrated by a girls team from Hamiota and a team from Baldur will show the best way to make a hat and how to trim it.

Babies were not ignored. A special babies clinic was established, manned by two doctors throughout the fair. Mothers were encouraged to bring their children in for an examination and advice on child-rearing. This early experiment in public health had an important purpose, spelled out clearly in a pre-fair advertisement:

If you live far from a doctor, and want your baby examined—if you wish to reassure yourself that your infant is perfectly normal and healthy—if your baby has some complaint which you do not understand—bring him to the baby clinic on the fair ground.

Hundreds of mothers, particularly from rural areas brought their children forward; many discovered their children needed medical attention.

The availability of such features and attractions only added to the obvious thrills and excitement generated by the midway and special features. The highlight of the 1921 show was unquestionably the daredevil antics of Mark Campbell, who performed acrobatics on a plane circling over the fair grounds. A number of bands, including the Cando band from North Dakota, played in front of the grandstand. Between horse races and cattle parades, an auto-polo event was staged on the racetrack infield. Specially-built Model T Fords, buttressed with metal cages to protect the riders, propelled the driver and "hitter" in a furious scramble around the field. There were other platform attractions, including the Ringers high-wire act, the Toyama Japanese balance troupe, the dancing Famous Cervene group, Jesse Blair Sterling and her Glasgow maids, specializing in Scottish dancing, and the "Farmer and His Pigs," which displayed the "wonderful tricks of his band of trained porkers."

Dominating the grounds was C. A. Wortham's midway. Such rides as Noah's Ark, Over the Falls, Mile-a-Minute Ride, and Dodge'm and attractions like auto racing, a water show, the tallest man and littlest man in the world, plus a variety of games and enticements filled out the grounds In 1921, 40 railway cars were required to bring the 400 actors, hucksters and shills who accompanied the exhibition carnival.

The 1921 exhibition also demonstrated the positive, and occasionally negative, relationship between the fair and the City of Brandon. The large and enthusiastic attendance illustrated the affection of city residents for the annual show. The active participation of local schools carried the added benefit of ensuring a ready audience in the form of doting mothers and fathers. The volunteer food booths were a vital part of the annual show. In 1921, the Women's Hospital Aid, Victoria Avenue Methodist Ladies Aid, Women's Auxiliary of St. George's Church, St. Matthew's Guild, and the Baptist Ladies Aid provided hot, "home-cooked" meals on the grounds. In addition, the "Willing Workers" of Knox Church provided dinners and suppers at two downtown locations each day of the fair. The community spirit of earlier years remained very much in evidence.

There were other signs, however, that all was not well. At the post-fair meetings of the Provincial Exhibition Association in 1918, concern was expressed that local businesses were gouging fair visitors. It appeared, upon investigation, that several hotels and restaurants in town had raised their prices for fair week, leaving fairgoers with a bad impression of Brandon business and with considerably lighter wallets. A comparison of prices with other exhibition centres reflected unfavorably on Brandon. The prob-

1925 June

"Just as the evening performance was about to begin in the trained wild animal circus tent on the Rubin and Cherry shows midway at the exhibition last night, pandemonium broke loose. As if by pre-arranged signal, every one of the 16 Nubian lions set up a deafening roaring "muggins," and the huge elephant trumpeted lustily and every caged animal howled. This deafening din attracted the attention of the keepers who rushed into the tent fearing trouble. Captain Dan Riley, the principal animal trainer, led the vanguard and arriving at the lions' cages, discovered the cause of the commotion, 'Alpha,' a beautiful lioness, had become a mother, giving birth to two tiny lion cubs and the rest of the menagerie were voicing their approval of the new arrivals.
from the *Brandon Sun*.

lem re-emerged in 1921. The *Brandon Sun* chastised the local businessmen:

> To invite guests in to a provincial fair and make an exhibition of our greed is injurious to our city's name and fame. The petty graft reaped by individuals in this way is permanent injury to the advance of the city. The very worst advertisement and most widely circulated bad name that a city can get is that from "gouging" its guests. Fair play's a jewel of an advertisement; "fair prices" should be fair prices.

The bad feelings generated by the actions of some local businesses, and by the city government, which raised streetcar fares just before the fair, could not dampen the enthusiasm for the 1921 exhibition. To most participants, fair-goers and commercial exhibitors, the fair was a pleasure. For the association and the entertainers, the exhibition was a smashing financial success. A pattern of successful exhibitions had been established in the first years after World War I which would carry through to the end of the decade.

The exhibition continued much the same through the 1920s, with only minor changes. Johnny J. Jones was soon back as the main midway attraction. Horse-pulling was held for the first time in 1924, as was the first Boys' Camp, held in conjunction with the Agricultural Extension Centre. Special contests—like a horse-shoeing event held in 1926—were tried, often found wanting, and dropped. Large bands were particularly popular in the 1920s. In 1926, the Coldstream Guards Band gave a series of well-attended concerts in front of the grandstand. The next year, the Australian National Band was brought in for the fair. The association was constantly trying to improve its show, an effort made challenging by the constant changes in fairgoers' interests.

Several standard features suffered from declining interests through the 1920s. Car races, which had attracted a huge audience the first few years they were held, fell from grace and were cancelled shortly after mid-decade. Even the horse-racing events, long a

57   *View of the midway, 1920.*

58 *Alex Stewart with "Dare Aspire," summer exhibition, c.1920.*

59 *Swine judging, Farm Boys' Camp, 1920.*

60 *A six-horse team in front of the grandstand.*

1926 18 May

The attractions committee approved a donation of $60 to members of the Kinsmen Club of Brandon who are taking a motorcade to Winnipeg to publicize the summer exhibition.

1926 2 July

"Robert Trout and Morice Willows, sixteen-year-old high school boys from Tulsa, Oklahoma, were visitors at the exhibiion on Thursday. They made the trip from their home on foot, with the exception of some "lifts" given them by generous-hearted travellers, to visit relatives in Alexander. It took them two weeks to make the journey. The boys were most enthusiastic about the fair which was the finest they had seen."

from the *Brandon Sun*.

main-stay attraction at the grounds, fell on hard times. In the early 1920s, fair organizers scrambled to add more races to the card, hoping to meet a seemingly insatiable demand for the events. By 1929, the saddle events were being phased out, with only two days of races held in 1929. Even the long-popular harness races suffered from declining attendance, and the exhibition association began to cut back on the prize money and the race schedule.

The distress in these few sections did not dampen the association management's enthusiasm or indicate any serious problem at the fair. All exhibition associations knew that their fairs lived or died according to their ability to keep up with changing demands and interests, and the alterations in the summer fair program simply reflected the efforts by the manager and directors to keep their rural and city audiences happy. They were pleased with what they produced, often bragging that their livestock entries and agricultural displays could compete with any in Canada, and proudly pointed to the fact that their grandstand performers had played at some of the largest exhibitions in the United States. The fair continued to change, sometimes upsetting traditionalists who liked things left as they were or always had been. But, by keeping up with changing trends in entertainment and agricultural competitions during the 1920s, the directors of the Provincial Exhibition of Manitoba ensured their place in the front rank of western Canadian exhibitions.

THE MANITOBA WINTER FAIR likewise maintained its position as a leading agricultural show. The decade did not prove to be one of dramatic change and the fair moved forward with extreme caution, staying with the format that had won it plaudits since the early 1900s. The winter fair lacked the excitement and attractions of the summer show; the absence of a midway and platform performers made it almost exclusively an agricultural presentation. The directors, thinking that the lack of entertainment detracted from attendance, hired singer Marjorie Wallace to perform at their 1918 evening show. But there was little desire to go much further for fear that this would detract from the agricultural components of the fair.

The winter fair began the decade with a solid performance. The 1920 fair attracted hundreds of entries. Over 300 cattle were on display; 76 boys had entered calves in the Boys' Fat Calf Competition; more than 150 horses participated in the various competitions. The Royal Canadian Mounted Police Musical Ride provided the highlight for the opening day ceremonies, a natural addition since the police horses were stabled in the Winter Fair arena year-round. There was no question that this was an agricultural show: cattle judging, heavy horse events, horse-jumping, a poultry show which boasted more than 4,000 entries and boys' competitions vied with educational programs and commercial displays for the attention of the fair-goers. Little entertainment was necessary, for the competitions themselves drew large crowds particularly for the heavy horse and jumping events.

The agricultural focus of the winter fair was a cause for both praise and concern. The applause came because the quality of the winter show gave substance to Brandon's claim as a prime agricultural centre. The concern was founded in the limited civic interest. The purpose of the event was education in the broadest possible sense of the word. Although obvious priority was placed on offering technical advice and encouragement to farmers, poultry men and cattle breeders, it was expected that the fair would also help introduce city dwellers to the work and accomplishments of the agricultural community. It did not appear to be working, for although attendance rose every year, the interest of Brandonites in attending the show seemed to be waning. One journalist commented in 1920,

There were hundreds of city people who were not inside the Arena. They lost the opportunity of seeing the finest array of livestock which has probably ever been assembled in Canada. They lost an opportunity to acquire knowledge along lines which every Canadian should possess. They failed to receive the inspiration which comes from the contemplation of achievements such as is only obtained through the application of scientific principles to the breeding of livestock.

The writer recommended that more entertainment be added to the nightly program, and that the fair management continue its efforts to keep the show running smoothly in order to prevent boredom. The success of the Musical Ride, he noted, demonstrated the need to combine agriculture with something more flashy than a stock parade. The directors of the Manitoba Winter Fair and Fat Stock Association would wrestle with this dilemma throughout the decade, but in general resisted the temptation to seek popular appeal at the expense of agriculture. A little more was done as years passed to liven up the proceedings, but in general the show remained an agricultural and educational event.

About seven months after the successful 1920 exhibition, the winter fair directors faced a major catastrophe. Through the summer, considerable work had been done on the old winter fair pavilion, the first structure erected by the association in 1908. On 20 October 1920, flames engulfed the structure. The mounted police, who lived in barracks near the building, and the local Fire Department responded to the alarm. The building was a tinderbox; its aged timbers and piles of straw provided natural fodder for the flames. The police and stable hands fought through the smoke in an attempt to rescue the 70 horses trapped inside. The large crowd which gathered applauded the mounties' brave attempts to re-enter the burning building, but the efforts were only partially successful. In all, 46 horses died in the blaze.

61 *Cover of the winter fair prize list, 1921.*

62 *Advertisement for Clydesdale horses in the 1921 winter fair prize list.*

The loss of the building, estimated at $125,000, threatened the 1921 Winter Fair. The first response of Manager W. I. Smale was to adopt an optimistic front and report confidently that a fair would be held on the summer fair grounds and that all records for attendance and entries would surely be broken. Even more, Smale and the directors asserted, the conflagration provided an opportunity to replace the aging structure with a modern new building which would make the Brandon Winter Fair the envy of all such fairs in the country.

The bravado could not mask the harsh realities which appeared as the smoke cleared and the damage was assessed. The directors discovered that insurance payments would cover less than $50,000 of the costs of a replacement building, estimated at between $100,000 and $200,000. There was discussion at the annual meeting of asking the provincial government to take over the facilities. J. D. McGregor rejected the suggestion on the grounds that it looked "too much as if we [are] crawling from under." While plans were discussed for the new building, the Manitoba Winter Fair Association decided that the 1921 show had to be cancelled. An effort was made to keep some smaller sections in operation. The poultry show was held at City Hall in February and in March the winter fair board hosted a much reduced stallion and fat-cattle show at the summer fair grounds.

A NEW WINTER FAIR BUILDING was a necessity and efforts proceeded towards that goal. Local architect David Marshall was commissioned to draft plans for a facility expected to cost close to $200,000. The two-storey building was designed to hold 300 horses on the main level, with stall space for cattle and a large display centre for poultry slated for the second floor. At the same time, work proceeded on an addition to the existing arena, adding more stable space and an improved marshaling area. The buildings were completed on schedule, and when fair-goers returned to the winter fair in March 1922, they got their first glimpse inside the new structure. The winter fair now had a first-rate showcase, easily among the best in the country.

The winter fair that year was a resounding success, as records for both attendance and entries were shattered. The directors had rebounded from the potentially devastating loss of the winter fair pavilion and had organized a top-quality show. The financial burden would linger for a number of years, as the Brandon Winter Fair board sought to pay off their heavy obligations. They achieved this in part by expanding on year-round use of their buildings. As early as 1913, the organization had rented out the arena for use as a skating rink; through the 1920s, they made several attempts to find a person or organization who could operate the facility profitably. C.G. Bennett and Murdoch McKenzie, both held the contract for one or more years, though more often the B.W.F.L.A. ran the facility itself. In addition, the rental of a portion of the arena to the Wheat City Curling Club brought in several hundred dollars a year. The total income was not great, but these measures did help offset the increasing financial difficulties facing the facility managers.

The dual-organization approach freed the Manitoba Winter Fair association to concentrate on the show itself, although interlocking directorships kept the two groups well aware of each others' activities. Though the participants understood their separate duties, the government apparently did not. Confusion over who actually merited the provincial agricultural grant in 1923 resulted in the grant not being paid on time, although a hasty representation by the Manitoba Winter Fair board ensured that the assistance was eventually forthcoming.

There were few changes in the fair itself. In 1917, poor crops had resulted in the cancellation of the annual seed grain exhibit. Though it was held again in 1920, the directors discovered, much to their dismay, that the Manitoba Seed Growers' Association had shifted their annual show to Winnipeg, where it failed to generate the audience expected. The Manitoba Winter Fair stepped in, offering premium display space in 1924 if the seed fair returned to Brandon, its natural home in the minds of many directors and fair-goers. The success of the 1925 Seed Fair resulted in an invitation to the seed men to keep their event in Brandon. The continuing interest in the show, and the obvious contribution the exhibit made to agricultural education, led the winter fair to consider a more permanent arrangement. In 1927, the association decided to amend its constitution to allow for representation of the seed growers on the board of directors, a sure sign that the Manitoba Winter Fair intended to maintain this fitting association.

Modifications to the winter fair prize lists also demonstrated changing attitudes and standards in the livestock industry. The 1920s witnessed the emergence of a strong anti-horn sentiment. The problem of gouging and boring was particularly acute when cattle were being shipped or massed together. The gathering of hundreds of expensive show cattle for the winter fair carried a severe threat of damage to animals if horned cattle were present. The winter fair directors declared in 1923 that "animals with horns on would be placed at a serious disadvantage at the 1925 and future fairs." This move was seconded by the stockyard companies and the federal department of agriculture, who similarly supported the initiative. At the 1927 annual meeting of the Manitoba Winter Fair Association, it was formally decided to go one step further. A motion passed declaring that "no horned cattle be eligible for exhibition at the Fairs conducted by this Association after the Annual Fair of 1928." One again sees the vital role of the exhibition as a leader in agricultural innovation. Those cattle breeders interested in showing their livestock would have to conform or lose this crucial opportunity to demonstrate the quality of their herd.

The winter fair, like the Provincial Exhibition, had clearly found its niche. Though a series of minor changes in format and organization were undertaken, the Manitoba Winter Fair and Fat Stock Association knew it had a winning formula. The ever-increasing number of entries, the obvious enthusiasm of the breeders, and the poultry, swine, sheep, horse and seed associations provided clear evidence that the winter fair was providing good service to the agricultural community. There were complaints, chiefly from those who favored more entertainment and a more conscious attempt to reach out to the urban audience, but they were constantly muted by the resounding applause for the work of the association.

Both of Brandon's fairs enjoyed expansion and public approval between 1913 and 1929. They were very different shows of course. The summer fair stressed entertainment, although prominent agricultural competitions, government displays and commercial exhibits provided for a well-rounded show. Still, the people came primarily for the midway, the platform shows, the horse races and the special grandstand performances. The directors were wise enough to recognize the needs and interests of the fair-goers and stuck with a program that was proving successful. The management of the winter fair also stayed with what worked, although their show appealed to a more specifically agricultural audience.

Brandon was suitably proud of the achievements of its two agricultural shows. The city had surrendered some of its more grandiose ambitions of urban growth by the 1920s, but clung to the belief that it was Manitoba's primary agricultural centre. The continued success of the Manitoba Winter Fair and the Provincial Exhibition of Manitoba provided irrefutable proof that the city was reaching out to its rural constituency and that in Brandon, unlike any other city in the province, the interests of town and country were intertwined. To this extent, the annual summer and winter fairs, both of which strove for a balance between the needs of its urban and rural constituencies, reflected well the struggle and accomplishments of the city itself.

63 *J.C. Donaldson, winter fair president, 1928-29. For years his firm promoted the fair by donating advertising time on CKX, Brandon, and CKDM, Dauphin.*

Chapter Three

1930 ‑ 1945

Years of Anxiety

🐦 *1929 19 August*
Hon. Winston Churchill
today was a visitor at the home
of Mr. and Mrs. J.D. McGregor.

By 1929, THE PROVINCIAL EXHIBITION OF MANITOBA and the Manitoba Winter Fair were at the forefront of the western Canadian exhibition movement. Through the previous decade, their directors had built on earlier successes, establishing a solid reputation of service to the agricultural community, and promoting the City of Brandon. The status gained in the past provided little preparation for the upheaval and difficult times that followed, however, for over the next 15 years, the directors of the two exhibition associations would have to guide their shows through a catastrophic Depression and a world war.

Most people point to the collapse of the New York stock market on 29 October 1929 as the beginning of the Depression in North America. The farmers and workers of western Canada knew better. The year 1928 had been a bumper one, with high crop yields and good prices; such prosperity would not soon be repeated. By mid-summer of the following year, the signs were ominous. Dry, hot weather killed the crops in the field. Farmers who ordinarily hired several laborers to help with the harvests held back. Those who had planned equipment purchases suspended their plans. The railway companies saw the impending crisis and began to lay off workers. All across the west, adjustments were made in anticipation of a poor crop. The expectations were not misplaced, for yields dropped to half of the previous year's returns. Thus began the great Depression in the west, that savage combination of drought, relief lines and unemployment that was to scar a generation.

Western Manitoba felt the full force of the gathering storm. Dust storms swirled through the region, blackening both the skies and peoples' hopes. The trains running through Brandon carried hundreds of unemployed, men fruitlessly searching for work and subsisting on the meagre offerings from soup kitchens and hand-outs. They were tough times for almost everyone. Faculty members at Brandon College accepted major reductions in their salaries, and even then the college seemed about to go under. City workers and railyard employees faced similar cuts in wages or outright

64   A crowd gathers for the evening grandstand presentation, c.1930.

lay-off. With the Province of Manitoba on the verge of bankruptcy, and the City of Brandon struggling to pay its rapidly escalating debts (and failing to do so in 1937), governments were scarcely in a position to provide much help.

It was an odd time even to contemplate an exhibition, for the frivolity and optimism of such a show appeared out of step with the desperate times. Brandon's summer and winter fairs had always stood for a prosperous future, and offered farmers help in achieving their dreams. All that seemed strikingly inappropriate now. But to the promoters of Brandon's two agricultural shows, their fairs were even more essential during the Depression. The shows directly helped farmers through troubled times, principally by encouraging excellence at a time when faith and enthusiasm were at a low ebb.

The entertainment aspect of the fairs, particularly the summer show, also had an important role to play. Through the 1920s, the summer spectacular had assumed an honored place in the lives of thousands of patrons. The annual trip to the fair was a family occasion, an irreplaceable highlight of the year. Certainly it was escapism, a chance to put the concerns of farm life away for at least a day, and that was exactly what the fair-goers wanted. Because of this, Brandon's summer fair, like many of the western Canadian shows, enjoyed surprising prosperity throughout the Depression, surprising only in that it stood out so sharply against the bleakness of the general economic pattern.

Although yearly attendance and profits stayed high through the 1930s, the fairs certainly reflected social problems. The economic strife of the decade was always present. In 1930, for example, the civic government requisitioned the winter fair buildings for use as temporary housing for the hundreds of unemployed men passing through the city. In 1935, relief camp workers protesting their living conditions and demanding meaningful jobs scheduled a cross-Canada march, the famous "On to Ottawa" trek. Advance men for the marchers requested permission to use the summer exhibition grounds as a temporary camp-site. The fair directors indicated their disapproval of what many businessmen viewed as a radical, or even Communist, escapade by turning down the request. The march never reached Brandon, having been dispersed in Regina on federal orders.

The fair boards dealt more kindly with the unemployed from their community. The winter fair directors repeatedly provided free admission to their show for those on relief. The Provincial Exhibition in 1934 similarly provided one-day passes to relief recipients who had worked on the grounds without pay over the summer. When a delegation from the Unemployed Ex-Service Men's League requested that the fair board give preference to its members when hiring for the summer show, the board promised to give those men preference when appropriate.

The summer fair had for a number of years hosted a baby clinic. During the Depression, many women who wanted their children examined could not afford the cost of admission. In 1933, the Provincial Exhibition Board asked one of its directors, S.E. Clement, to investigate the requests of 12 women and, if their cases warranted, to provide free tickets.

THE EXHIBITION DIRECTORS soon discovered a hidden silver lining amid the clouds of Depression. Although their own limited resources would not allow major expenditures on repairs and ground work, relief recipients were readily available as workers. The city government, for example, provided its annual grant to the summer fair on the condition that the exhibition adopt the "Fair Wage Schedule"—something it had avoided in the past— and hire Brandon's unemployed as much as possible. The wage rates were hardly generous, only $3.00 per day, and the board still had to be pressured to comply. The move by the city government did, however, provide some measure of help for the disadvantaged.

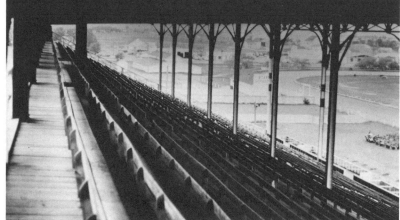

65 *Displays of the Manitoba Department of Agriculture, and the Manitoba Agricultural College, at the 1930 summer exhibition.*

66 *The interior of the grandstand, c.1930.*

94

The various levels of government believed, even in the depths of the Depression, that people receiving relief had to work for their pay lest they find life on the dole too attractive. A variety of public works were undertaken as special relief projects. Both the Provincial Exhibition and the Manitoba Winter Fair received government grants to improve their facilities. The summer fair board requested that the provincial government pay for repairs to the grandstand as an authorized relief project; approval was given for reconstruction work estimated to cost $40,000. A similar federal grant of $25,000 in 1936 allowed for much-needed repairs to the winter fair buildings. The summer fair board tried again in 1937. Fair manager J.E. Rettie approached the deputy minister of agriculture and the secretary of the Social Service and Employment Service Commission while in Ottawa and gained their approval for further work on the grounds. This grant under the National Employment Works' Scheme paid for the extension of city water services to the fair grounds and the demolition of the old Crystal Palace, some of the wood from which was used as flooring in the Automobile Building. In addition, the fair boards received smaller grants on a regular basis which allowed them to hire unemployed men on make-work projects, like grounds clean-up and general painting. The use of relief workers in western Canada often involved a scandalous abuse of their labor and misuse of their talents, and the exhibition projects were no exception. In these instances at least, their work was being turned to productive use in aid of important civic institutions.

As the municipal, provincial and federal governments wrestled with the seemingly insoluble problem of massive unemployment, they found themselves unable to meet their regular financial obligations. For the summer and winter fairs, this meant an endless series of reductions or cancellations of their grants. The Rural Municipality of Oakland regretfully cancelled its annual contribution to the summer fair in 1931; the R.M. of Cornwallis reduced their grant to $50.00 in 1934. Ottawa's cuts hurt the most, largely

1930 14 February
The continuing interest of the public in morality on the midway is a matter of constant concern to exhibition directors. This interest extends even to the characters in a wax museum. At today's meeting of the exhibition board, a letter was read from E.L. Richardson, Calgary, who requested that the Morris and Castle Carnival be asked "to limit the figures in the wax show to those of people who have held honorable positions in life."

1930 11 April
The exhibition board debated a letter from S.W. Johns, commenting on the opinion of R. James Speers, the racing organizer, on the subject of race-track tipsters.
Mr. Speers believes that "instead of warning the public against characters of this nature that we employ a plain-clothes detective and have any such characters run off the grounds, and where the evidence would warrant it, arrested."

because the agricultural shows counted so heavily on the federal assistance for their prize lists. The Department of Agriculture cut its annual grant to the winter fair in half in 1932, dropping it from $5,000 to $2,500, and eliminated its support for special competitions. The loss of revenue almost forced the winter show to close, although a last minute $1,000 increase in the subsidy convinced the directors to carry on. The problems did not end there. The federal government, on occasion, was slow in delivering its grant; in 1935, it came so late that the fair was unable to pay out all the prize money on time.

The summer fair's difficulties with federal and provincial grants caused hardship, but this show was much less dependent on government assistance. In 1932, the federal government threatened to eliminate all grants to Class "A" fairs, a move which would have virtually destroyed the prize lists. Organized protests against the move convinced the government to pay half the usual subsidy, and in 1935 the grants were returned to the original level. The Province of Manitoba, itself teetering on the verge of bankruptcy, similarly cut back its allocations for fairs. The minister of agriculture announced in 1934 that such grants were being eliminated. Secretary-manager J.E. Rettie, and directors N.W. Kerr and Edward Fotheringham approached the minister to protest the changes. But as Rettie reported to the association later,

> This could not be achieved without drastically reducing public school grants. When it was found necessary to do this, it was decided that all grants except the balance of those to public schools and hospitals would have to be eliminated. He did not think it would be possible to have the grant for the Provincial Exhibition reinstated without including that for Portage, Dauphin and Carmen, stating that it would not likely pass the house.

Premier John Bracken had no money to offer, but he did have some hopeful words. As Rettie wrote, the Premier "urged us to carry on for this year, feeling that another year assistance might be granted."

The provincial grants were no more forthcoming in subsequent years as the grip of the Depression tightened on the west. Even the City of Brandon began to withdraw its financial support. In 1936, the promised city grant for the Provincial Exhibition did not arrive as scheduled, forcing the board to consider defaulting on its debenture interest. The exhibition had little of its own money to offset the declining government assistance. Its inability to meet its tax obligations on several lots next to the fair grounds led to the appearance of those properties on the city's 1931 tax sale list. The threat to sell the land for taxes owing convinced the association to negotiate a suitable financial deal with the councillors.

The Manitoba Winter Fair Association had always been on a shaky financial footing, and the loss of the grants left the show in an extremely vulnerable position. It was almost exclusively an agricultural show, and without sizable prize lists the show was hardly worth staging. The reduction in prize lists brought understandable results. Farmers and breeders were not likely to prepare their entries of cattle, poultry, swine or seeds without a reasonable prospect of reward. For many, the Depression was not a time to compete just for the pleasure of participating. The prize money which in the 1920s had averaged $23,000 paid to the winners among 1800 entries, within 10 years had shrunk to $7,500 and the number of entries had decreased by half.

While the directors of the two Brandon fairs understood the necessity of these reductions in grant money, they also believed, somewhat naively, their shows were vital in encouraging the kind of agricultural innovation that would lift the west out of the Depression. They interpreted the lack of support from federal and provincial governments as a sign of limited confidence in the work of their associations.

The railway companies also suffered from the downturn in the agricultural economy, and this altered their relationship with the fairs. For years, the excursion trains had been the lifeline of the Brandon summer fair. A regular schedule of "excursion

Our Exhibit at the Fair

Is very convenient for meeting with your friends.

We invite you to make it your headquarters.

Full line of Seeding, Haying and Harvesting Machines, also Tractors, Motor Trucks, Cream Separators and Binder Twine.

International Harvester Company

OF CANADA LIMITED

Office Phone 2311 Repairs Dept. Phone 4003

Brandon, Man.

1930

Members of Teck Chapter IODE and Brandon Kinsmen were just two of the organizations providing direct assistance to exhibition visitors during the early 1930s. IODE members operated a day nursery where infants could be cared for; the Kinsmen provided the volunteer staff for a "well baby" clinic which operated two hours each morning and three hours each afternoon. Medical specialists and nurses examined the children free of charge and provided the mothers with advice on health and nutrition.

1930 16 June

A letter was read from D.R.P. Coates with reference to Uncle Peter announcing that the Peterkins would be given admission to the grounds if they were wearing their badges. It was decided to write Mr. Coates that our intention was that this should apply for Monday, June 30th, Children's Day only, and that we would not be able to add any additional features to our program.
from the minutes.

1930 15 July

Mr. McKenzie King today was a visitor at the home of Mr. and Mrs. J.D. McGregor.

67 *From the 1935 Exhibition program.*

ಠಿ *1932 4 July*

A news story tells that a WAR TIME DUGOUT ATTRACTS INTEREST. Near the north entrance of the provincial building there was a dugout from "somewhere in France." ..."The whole lay-out is the work of the local branch of the Canadian Legion, who have prepared it as a gesture of goodwill to the many ex-servicemen who will gather at the fair grounds on Warriors' Day..."
from the *Brandon Sun.*

ಠಿ *1933 3 July*

A sad commentary on the state of the economy may be read in the exhibition minutes of this date.

"Mr. Clement stated that there were about 12 women from families who are on relief who wished to have their babies examined at the Baby Clinic conducted by the public health nurses in the Health Building, and that they had no funds to pay admission to the grounds." Mr. Clement was authorized to issue 'helpers' tickets' to those cases of genuine need.

68   *Hard times force prairie men to drift, like their topsoil, with the winds of the day.*

specials," offered at greatly reduced prices, brought fair-goers from eastern Manitoba, North Dakota, and Saskatchewan to Brandon. W.J. Quinlan, district passenger agent for Canadian National Railways, informed the Provincial Exhibition in 1931 that the special trains had been cancelled. The other railways followed suit. The fairs fought back, for they knew the special trains brought in hundreds of competitors and thousands of spectators. Lengthy negotiations extracted a concession from the railway companies; instead of special trains, they offered a return ticket for the price of a single fare, with a two-day time limit, on all branch lines leading to Brandon and on the Canadian Pacific mainline to Broadview. This was later changed to a standard charge of one cent per mile for visitors to the fair, a rate that was comparable to the earlier excursion fare.

Although the financial arrangements were satisfactory, the elimination of the excursion trains proved to be a major blow. Many spectators and competitors still came, but only on regularly scheduled trains, and the excitement of this "exhibition special" was gone. The sense of being part of something unique had been eliminated. The railways doubtlessly saved a great deal of money; it was easier to add a few cars to the regular train than to lay on an extra excursion. But the elimination of the special trains, and their replacement with some sterile concessions on the passenger rates, had taken some of the heart out of the summer show.

PERHAPS THE MOST STARTLING ASPECT of the summer and winter fairs during the Depression is how little things actually changed. Squabbles with governments over grants and prize lists may have concerned agricultural exhibitors and fair directors, but few spectators noted any significant differences from the shows which during earlier years had won uniform acclaim.

The 1933 summer exhibition exemplified the quiet success of the Depression fairs. The headlines did not scream excitedly as they had in the past; such transparent optimism seemed decidedly out of place in those sombre times. The fair opened on 3 July, in blazing heat. Hundreds of children crowded through the entrance gates to take advantage of the special prices on Children's Day. The sale of strip tickets—four for $1 rather than the standard 50 cents each—promised to swell attendance above that of the previous year.

The day which began with such promise ended with the promises unrealized. The full house which gathered in the grandstand to view the "Birds of Paradise" revue presented by Castle-Erhlick Shows had to dash for cover shortly after the opening fanfare. Sudden heavy rain and strong winds damaged a number of tents and midway shows. Employees worked all night repairing the damage.

The rest of the week went better. The addition of a daily attendance draw, held during the night-time grandstand show, added further excitement to the 1933 proceedings. The prizes were impressive. The winner the first day took home a Shetland pony; the grand prize winner, Miss Sadie Bertram, took home a Plymouth automobile on the final day. As one observer noted :

> As the young lady presented the right ticket and was awarded the car, thousands of sheets of papers containing nearly 244,000 numbers fluttered from the hands of expectant car-owners.

By all accounts, the draw increased attendance and also added significantly to the evening crowd in the grandstand.

The show they witnessed was typical of the grandstand extravaganzas that toured the Class "A" circuit. A brilliantly-colored backdrop established the theme. Ballet dancers, comic skits and musical performances warmed up the audience. The crowd thrilled to a tumbling act by the Eight Toyama Japs and the high wire performance of the Seven Tip Tops. It was an odd assembly, although one particularly suited to the grandstand stage. The large crowds and enthusiastic response suggested that the fair directors had selected another winning performance.

Few spectators reached the grandstand without first navigating the "Gladway" filled with rides, games of chance and shows. In 1933, the midway included Roxie the fire-fighting horse, Russian, Spanish and Oriental dancers, a "Safe in Hell" exhibit which "depicts the results of crime and is really an educational exhibit," and a variety of other treats for the curious and the gullible.

The midway attracted much attention and most of the money, but there was far more to do at the fair. A baseball tournament featuring teams from the Brandon area attracted an enthusiastic following. The Canadian Legion erected a mock trench, designed to depict warfare in France. The display provided an excellent counterpart to "Warriors Day," at which time World War I veterans from the Western Manitoba region were invited to visit the grounds and register at a special booth put up to honor them. An impressive horticultural show and a seemingly endless series of cattle, swine and poultry displays and competitions provided hours of entertainment. The aging Crystal Palace, once the cornerstone of the display buildings but now in rough shape, played host to an impressive number of corporate displays. Many of the companies involved were local firms, including Brandon Heating and Plumbing, Mechlair's Furs, Wheat City Cereal, Kullberg's Furniture, and the Humid Heater Manufacturing Company.

Observers agreed that the 1933 fair had been an artistic success; a review of the books after all the accounts were in revealed a handsome profit. It was a understated event. The optimism and boosterism of the 1920s were understandably absent. The message of the fair seemed to be that the future would be better, although that message was not projected with much confidence. The fair came and went, thousands attended, tens of thousands of dollars were spent, and the entertainers provided hours of pleasure. Still, the pall of the Depression was hard to escape, and even though the big show offered a brief respite from the most dreary of times, the distress was evident everywhere.

1933

Exhibition Week

"Professor" Jerome advertises in the Brandon Sun that in his tent "near the entrance to the midway," he offers farm patrons his services as the "world's foremost astrologer, psychologist, renowned palmist, character reader, and expert adviser on social and personal problems."

69 *The midway of the Johnny J. Jones Exposition, c. 1930.*

70 *The 1935 exhibition featured a competitive rodeo for the first time.*

Through the rest of the depression, the management of the Provincial Exhibition tried a number of gimmicks to increase attendance and protect themselves from financial disaster. The strip tickets proved popular, and the car draw on the final day became a big event. The Provincial Exhibition ran into difficulties when it attempted to turn the ticket sale into a lottery. The idea was simple enough. Tickets were available at a reduced price through the mail. Major prizes, including automobiles and trips were offered as an incentive. In actual fact, the tickets, many of which were never used, were used as a cover for the draw. The event was tried in 1936 and was apparently successful. When the winter fair tried the same device that year, it ran afoul of government regulations and the advance sale scheme had to be dropped.

Beyond these attempts to finance the fair through ticket sales, the directors made few substantial changes in the show over the next decade. A special effort was made to organize a "Made in Manitoba" exhibit. Reduced railway freight rates were secured for exhibitors displaying Manitoba-produced goods. However, this laudable ambition attracted few entries, and the fair was forced to open up the display building set aside for provincial manufacturers to Brandon firms, at reduced rates. Even the Automobile Building, erected to such acclaim only a few years earlier, could not be filled with exhibitors, and after the car companies' initial contracts lapsed, the building stood all but empty. The board kept hoping in vain that a resurgence in the auto industry would increase their exhibits, but it did not come and the building fell into disuse. After standing empty for a few seasons, in 1939 it was turned into a cafeteria.

Demands for change focused, rather oddly, on the exhibition board itself. Unlike the winter fair board, which included a number of breed association representatives, the exhibition directors were virtually a closed shop. They were elected at an annual general

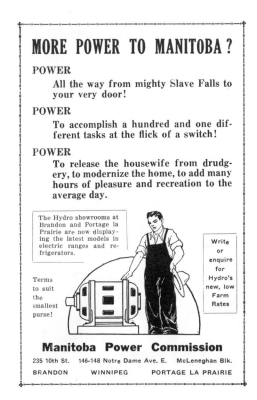
71 *Encouragement of electrification—from the 1935 Exhibition Prize List.*

72 *J.W. Reid, winter fair president 1930-31.*

73 *James Turner, exhibition president, 1935-36, winter fair president, 1941-46.*

meeting. While the "rules of order" provided opportunities to unseat existing directors and select new leadership, in practice, little actually changed from year to year. Local residents knew that winning entry to the select group was a difficult challenge. This concentration of leadership posed the possibility of the group continuing as a self-sustaining clique.

There were few abuses of office, few indications that the directors were indeed using their office for personal pecuniary benefit. The opposite was closer to the truth, for the directors provided freely of their time and were often called on to make financial contributions. But the system was not pristine. In 1940, for example, the board distributed the largest share of its insurance contracts to companies represented by board members.

Although the problems were more apparent than real, the composition of the board became the focus for opposition. At the 1933 annual meeting of the Provincial Exhibition, two slates of candidates were brought forward to compete with the existing directors. A large crowd filled the city council chambers, and placed some pointed questions on the table. The discontented shareholders accused the directors of losing touch with agriculture and ignoring the needs of the livestock industry. Long-time director N.W. Kerr was obviously concerned with the electoral threat to the association:

> "For years it has been said that the Board of Directors are annually elected by the Old Directors and their friends, that new blood is not infused into the organization by reason of this practice....Each of these slates—and I make no reference to myself—omits the names of one or more 1932 Directors who are amongst the most energetic and hardworking Directors on your Board...[In] my humble opinion your institution cannot be run by slates or cliques, that today as never before your organization, like other organizations, needs men of vision and initiative."

There were forty-four nominations for the twenty positions on the board, and when the ballots were counted seven new members took their seats at the directors' table.

While the accusations of 1933 still hung in the air, another internal dispute rocked the organization the year following. Although the details remain unclear, long-time director Kerr raised some serious questions concerning the performance of manager J.E. Rettie. Rettie responded to Kerr's comments, but Kerr remained unconvinced and immediately resigned from the board. A vote of confidence in Rettie was called, and passed 10 to 8. That decision caused two additional directors, Dowling and Fotheringham, to tender their resignations. Other directors tried to get the three to reconsider, but they refused and eventually were replaced.

Kerr, Fotheringham and Dowling could not stay away from the fair for long, however, and were re-elected the following year. Their displeasure with past management practices continued. At a 14 September 1936 meeting, Kerr and Fotheringham asked for a report on all cheques of $500 or more issued during the week of 6-11 July. It is not clear what they were after, but immediately following the manager's report on the matter, Fotheringham moved that "J.E. Rettie be advised that it was the intention of the Board to dispense with his services after due notice." That proposal failed, although an amendment that the question be deferred to the annual meeting was accepted. At the next regular meeting, Kerr, Dowling and Fotheringham again tendered their resignations and again refused to stand for re-election. The records do not indicate the nature of the discontented members' disappointment with Rettie, although the manager stayed and the dissidents were eventually induced to come back on the board.

LIFE FOR THE MANITOBA WINTER FAIR was only marginally less tumultuous. The decline in government subsidies severely damaged the prize lists and forced the association to scramble to keep their fair in operation. At several points, the directors considered

ॐ 1936 6 November
At the exhibition meeting, a letter was read from H.W. Thornborough who applied to purchase a share in the association. In the same letter Mr. Thornborugh solicited the directors for a part of the insurance business for the coming year. According to the minutes, "This was referred to the new board without either motion or dissent."

ॐ 1936 16 December
At the meeting of exhibition directors, approval was given for the purchase of automobiles to be used as admission prizes. A Chevrolet "master coach," complete with trunk was ordered for $820. The matching Plymouth was ordered at $920; the Dodge cost $933.

COME TO THE FAIR

EVERYTHING IS SET FOR AN EXCITING WEEK !

MONDAY---DOMINION and WARRIOR'S DAY

Draw for Chesterfield Suite . . . Bring Your Merchant Gift Tickets!

HARNESS RACES
MONDAY, WEDNESDAY AND THURSDAY AFTERNOONS
PARI-MUTUEL SYSTEM OF BETTING.

TUESDAY---"CHILDREN'S DAY"
BABY COMPETITION   DOLL PARADE   and   CONTESTS

SOFTBALL TOURNAMENT and THRILLING
BICYCLE and TRACTOR RACES
Featuring the renowned Allis Chalmers; "999" tractors driven by the world famous driver Lou Meyer and other well known speed track pilots.

DRAW for BICYCLE TUESDAY AFTERNOON

SEE and HEAR
TELEVISION
The Wonder of the Age; and
"ALPHA" the robot
The wonderful mechanical man.

Gorgeous Grandstand Attractions
"THE SHOW OF A CENTURY"
A spectacular musical production to be presented each evening in front of the Grandstand. Beautiful girls, marvellous scenic and lighting effects, novelties, original dances, enthralling music; unexcelled entertainment for young and old.

BAND FESTIVAL, FRIDAY, JULY 6th.
SPECIAL RAILWAY RATES.

DRAW FOR VALUABLE ATTENDANCE PRIZES
IN FRONT OF GRANDSTAND EACH AFTERNOON.

74   *An advertisement from Brandon Daily Sun, June 1934. One of the features was a television display.*

cancelling the show for lack of funds, But they continued, often supporting the event out of their own pockets. They also tried a number of new inducements to improve attendance.

The winter fair board discovered that the advance ticket system used by the summer fair would work for them as well. A first draft of the scheme called for the sale of a strip of four tickets for $1.00. It was soon found that the addition of prizes increased public interest. In a move strikingly appropriate for the winter fair, the prizes for 1936 were set as 130 bushels of No. 2 Northern wheat (valued at $100.00), with lesser prizes for the four other winners.

The modest success encouraged the directors to adopt the more grandiose scheme used that summer by the Provincial Exhibition. The winter fair board paid $300 for the summer fair's mailing list and offered autombiles as prizes in an effort to increase sales. Tickets were printed and plans proceeded for an aggressive campaign which the directors believed could solve their financial problems. Then the government stepped in, seized the winter fair's mail, and announced that plans to sell the tickets by mail were illegal. The manager travelled to Ottawa in a desperate attempt to salvage the project. He was informed the association's mail would be released only if they:

> "...cancel the prize feature of our advance ticket sale campaign and give an understanding to write to every person who remitted or might remit for these tickets."

The order that the money be refunded almost emptied the winter fair's general account. The entire operation had to be scrapped at the last minute, at considerable cost to the cash-starved association.

The winter fair suffered from a major deficiency which the directors tried repeatedly to rectify. Unlike the summer show, which offered a vast array of rides, games and attractions, the winter fair was almost exclusively a livestock, poultry and seed show. Although the emphasis on livestock was praiseworthy, it did not attract large crowds. This problem was compounded during the Depression, by declining attendance and reduced government grants. Something had to be done to build the audience.

The board in 1930 hired the Welsh Brothers trick riders to liven up the proceedings, but their performance floundered when the bucking broncos refused to buck. In subsequent years, groups like the Elliott Family Orchestra, Peter Pan Dancing Club, YMCA gymnasts, clowns, Scotch and Irish Dancers, Cambridge Stables Horse Acts and other local performers were booked. By the late 1930s, a rather standard program of local acts, highlighting the Ukrainian Dancers, Brandon Boys' Pipe Band and dancers from Earl Haig School had become standard fare. It was a fine opportunity to involve Brandon people in the annual event, but it attracted few extra spectators, except the parents and family of the young performers.

The centre ring entertainment was supplemented through this period with a variety of other acts. The Lord Strathcona Horse performed its mounted drills and rides at several fairs, as did the Winnipeg Light Horse Club, which presented a popular hunting scene. The heavy-horse teams, always a popular feature, were highlighted in 1934 and 1935. In the first instance, a "popularity contest" was held; the following year, a driving competition was substituted, to the audience's acclaim. In 1934, the directors also included an auto parade and style show, with entries from many of Brandon's leading stores and car dealers. These innovations represented the directors' continuing attempts to broaden the appeal of their show, and in particular to attract more city-dwellers to a farm show.

The winter board also learned the necessity of working with the local community during the Depression years. The "Dirty Thirties" were tough times for most western Canadians, and Brandon and district were not spared the economic distress. A number of local institutions neared financial ruin. In 1934, the

75   *Keith Macpherson at the summer fair, 1934.*

76   *An admission ticket for the 1937 summer show. When postal authorities accused the directors of contravening the law by mailing lottery tickets, the board responded with a ticket which offered to "sell" the winners their prizes for $1.00.*

77   *Lil Macpherson and Betty Wilkes are shown on 11th Street between the Armoury and the Wheat City Arena. They are driving W.F. McRae's team, an entry in the 1936 winter fair.*

support of local service clubs, including the Board of Trade, Kiwanis Club, Rotary Club and Kinsmen Club was recruited to assist with the sale of tickets, a practise continued in subsequent years. Also in 1934, the winter board received the help of the Industrial Development Board in finding appropriate tenants for their display space. This cooperation may not have saved the winter fair, but the board discovered much needed local support for their efforts and found that the citizens and businessmen of Brandon were surprisingly interested in ensuring the continued success of the important agricultural event. The lesson was well learned. The Depression had brought the community and the winter fair together as never before, and the board was determined to keep this connection intact.

The annual shows in this decade continued to lack the spark and excitement which characterized the summer extravaganza. The 1933 event was typical of the low-key, but highly professional fairs staged by the Manitoba Winter Fair and Fat Stock Association. The barns and stables were filled to capacity, a suitable prize list had been arranged, and the judges were selected. A gala opening ceremony, presided over by the Honorable D.G. MacKenzie, Minister of Agriculture, got the fair off to a good start. The daily events consisted of cattle judging, heavy horse competitions and a variety of jumping events. The junior farmers were well-represented in the boys' and girls' calf competitions. A number of commercial, educational and school displays were on view, although this part of the show was only a modest imitator of the summer exhibition.

The events in the main arena, a far cry from the grandstand shows of the summer fair, nonetheless attracted a fair-sized crowd. The Thursday night schedule, slated as the highlight of the week's events, called for a parade of prize-winning horses and cattle, competitions for hunting horses, single pony in harness, the ever-popular four-horse and six-horse teams, heavy harness horses and a horse-jumping exhibition. Between events, performances by

꙰ 1937 25 June

At the exhibition meeting the directors were advised that because of a difference of opinion between the exhibition and the postal authorities concerning the distribution of lottery tickets, drastic action had been taken by the postal authorities. As of that day, "A general order had been issued that any mail going out in our name or addressed to us must be intercepted and sent to the Dead Letter Office at Ottawa..." As a result of Mr. Rettie's successful intervention with the deputy postmaster general, this order was partially rescinded. "Arrangements were made that our mail would be delivered, provided it was opened in the presence of a post office official and any tickets on the car draw or any money connected thereto be turned over to the postal authorities."

78   *H.A. McNeill, exhibition president, 1937-1940, a Brandon barrister.*

the Peter Pan Dancing Club and a Ukrainian dance troupe enlivened the proceedings. Those truly interested in livestock and agriculture, and there were many, could find much to entertain them. Anyone straying into the winter fair buildings in search of the thrills and excitement of a summer fair, however, would likely be disappointed.

Although the 1933 fair experienced a substantial decline in attendance from the previous year, the directors still claimed success. The minister of agriculture proclaimed that "Nothing is doing so much to increase the standard of excellence of our livestock than the Manitoba winter fair." A number of agricultural associations, including the Manitoba Seed Growers, Manitoba Poultry Association and the Manitoba Cattle Breeders Association held their annual conventions in conjunction with the fair, adding to the opportunities to promote the development and prosperity of the west's ailing agricultural sector.

Even these harsh times produced entries and competitors worthy of recognition. L.J. Mitchell of Roblin carried off the top prize in the seed-growing competition. Also impressive was the performance of Perpetual Nugget, owned and shown by William McDonald of Brookdale. Like most other competitors in the boys' and girls' competitions, McDonald entered his 910-pound Aberdeen Angus calf in the open competitions as well. The young exhibitor received top prize of $60 in the boys and girls competition, a $50 special bonus from the Aberdeen Angus Association, a further $25 from that group for having the top entry in the entire cattle show, $15 for the best calf in its class, and $35 for winning the calf pairs with another Brookdale animal. In addition, the T. Eaton company purchased the animal for 25 cents a pound, bringing $227.50 for the animal. All together, young McDonald's winnings totaled $412.50, a handsome prize at any time, but doubly so during the Depression.

The directors had done their best to produce a top-flight winter fair for the 1933 season. They were disappointed in the poor attendance, but pleased with the quality of the entries and competition. The politicians praised the event, regretting only that financial troubles prevented them from being more generous. The 1933 fair proved typical of the Depression shows, struggling by on a bare-bones budget and sustained by the continuing support of the breed and agricultural associations. The fair even provided an excellent forum and large audience for the local performers. The directors wanted their event to be agricultural in purpose and substance, and there was little included in the program to detract from that emphasis.

BOTH THE SUMMER AND WINTER FAIRS emerged from the Depression intact. The Provincial Exhibition fared better, largely because its focus on entertainment provided a much-needed escape from the pervasive dreariness of the Thirties. The continuing decline in government support, justified by the financial crisis then rocking the nation, hurt the agricultural competitions somewhat but did not deter the fair organizers. Both the Provincial Exhibition and the Manitoba Winter Fair defined their central purpose as the encouragement of the basic industry. Both survived the Depression, but the end of the economic distress brought little joy, for the horrors of war had taken its place.

Canada officially declared war on Germany on 10 September 1939. Almost overnight, the money and government commitment necessary to prosecute the war effort was mobilized. The hordes of unemployed who had criss-crossed the country for 10 years in search of work now joined the rapidly lengthening line-ups at the recruiting depots. Farmers were urged to provide food for the armed forces and for the Allies. There was excitement, and fear, as the young men and women volunteered for overseas service and as people on the home front prepared to support them.

79 *Robert Macpherson, Carl Roberts, and Archie Macpherson, stand in front of what the winter fair directors described as a "million-dollar Percheron exhibit," 1938.*

80 *Holstein cattle class at the exhibition, 1938.*

This massive national commitment obviously demanded a great deal from all people and all regions. The west retained its traditional role as bread-basket, but there were changes that brought the war much closer to home than during World War I. Rural and town families each evening followed the war news, listening to the chilling broadcasts from the BBC in London, after which the sombre voice of Lorne Green told Canadians about the efforts of the troops overseas. These broadcasts gave the war a sense of immediacy the first World War had lacked two decades earlier. Westerners could not escape the trauma; there were simply too many reminders of Canada's major, on-going assistance to the Allied effort in Europe and the Pacific.

Exhibitions and fairs in western Canada could scarcely be expected to be immune from the new demands. During World War I, the government had recognized that exhibit buildings provided excellent facilities for mobilization and training of troops, storage of equipment and other military uses. In 1939, the federal government moved quickly to appraise the buildings and grounds held by the nation's exhibitions.

A number of western Canadian exhibitions gave up their property and were forced either to pare down or cancel their summer shows. In 1940, the Central Canada Exhibition in Ottawa had to close. Regina and Saskatoon in 1941 surrendered most of their grounds to the Department of National Defence, but declared their determination to continue their shows. Edmonton gave up most of their buildings that same year, but continued with a reduced fair until 1943, when they cancelled entirely. Vancouver's exhibition held out until 1942, when the grounds were taken over to provide space for the thousands of Japanese-Canadians being removed from the coastal defence zone to the British Columbia interior. Once the grounds were surrendered, the government retained control until 1946, forcing the cancellation of five consecutive shows. Also in 1942, the Canadian National Exhibition in Toronto shut its doors as the military moved in.

81   *H.L. Singleton, summer fair director and past-president, 1938-1940. Mr. Singleton was proprietor of Brandon Heating and Plumbing Ltd.*

82,83 *Two advertisements enticing patrons to the 1940 fair.*

84   *Entrants in the 1940 winter fair. Jim Evans on Dr. Rhythm, Gracia Gray on Sunshine, Betty Reid on Dr. Dan, Lil Hedman on Firefly, Lil Macpherson on Saratoga, Audrey MacArthur on Buster.*

85   *Ad for the 1940 Exhibition—from the June, 1940, Brandon Daily Sun.*

86   *Provincial Exhibition board of directors, 1941.*
First row:
A.G. Buckingham,
W.A. Cameron, (unidentified),
Miss B.M. Benson, Roy Clark,
W.W. Rathwell.
Second row:
J.E. MacArthur, W. Davidson,
H.M. Clark.
Third row:
H.L. Singleton, Isaac Cormick,
E. Fotheringham, N.W. Kerr,
W.U. Pitfield, P.A. McPhail.
Fourth row:
A.C. Pearson, G. Fitton,
W.A. Prugh, J.I. Moore,
H.F. Washington,
H.A. McNeill.
Back row:
J.C. Donaldson,
W.L. McGregor, C.S. Unicume,
Joe Taylor, James Turner.

113

THE PROVINCIAL EXHIBITION OF MANITOBA bucked this trend and kept the summer show open throughout the war. This did not mean that it escaped unscathed. As early as August 1940, the Department of National Defence asked to lease a parking lot east of the grounds for use as a military camp. The directors agreed, and patriotically rented the property to the government for $1 for the duration. By the fall of that year, a request had been received for the use of the summer fair grounds by the 101st Militia Training Centre. An agreement was quickly reached, which called for the army to return the property as required each year for fair purposes. The next year, the Royal Canadian Air Force offered to rent a number of minor exhibition buildings. The exhibition agreed again, finding in the monthly rental fees a revenue which protected the fair from financial problems.

Although the Provincial Exhibition directors were understandably careful not to appear unpatriotic, they were also careful to protect their annual show. In September 1942, the A-4 Artillery Training Centre approached the fair with a request for several buildings. The directors composed a carefully worded rejection, complete with a patriotic rider. Their answer declared that they:

> ...had seriously considered the request, and while we are willing to co-operate in any responsible way with your department, we feel that your occupation would result in our being obliged to discontinue our annual exhibition, and consequently hesitate to grant your request. If, however, it is the view of the department on account of the necessity of the situation that space and grounds are indispensable, we will, on definite word from you, give the matter our further careful consideration.

The directors collectively held their breath, hoping that their show would not fall victim to the government's need for training and storage space. They were ultimately successful in maintaining control of their grounds and therefore in keeping the fair in operation.

There was another threat which hung over the exhibition throughout the war. While they continued to control their facilities, the directors had access to fewer attractions. Conklin Shows in 1941 had won the Class "A" exhibition contract for the west. Carl J. Sedlmayr tried in 1942 to bring his Royal American shows, a fixture in the west since the 1930s, back to the prairies, but restrictions on cross-border transportation prevented him from doing so.

The limited competition soon appeared to be the least of the Brandon fair's problem. War-time pressures placed tremendous demands on the Canadian transportation system. The government imposed strict controls and reduced the space allocated to "non-essential" business. To the horror of fair directors across the west, Patty Conklin discovered in 1943 that his carnival train had been designated "non-essential." The western fairs banded together to lobby the federal government, particularly James Gardiner, minister of agriculture. Gardiner's intervention permitted Conklin to transport his supplies by regular freight. The problem was not completely solved; Conklin could only get space for half the equipment he intended to bring west and his show suffered accordingly.

These problems aside, the exhibition continued. It was a different show, tied specifically to the themes and needs of the war. Beginning with the 1940 exhibition, the directors attempted to convince the military authorities to schedule special military maneuvers during the fair. Such a spectacle would, it was believed,:

> "be greatly appreciated by the people both from the standpoint of entertainment as well as educational in so far as giving them an idea of something of the general training being given the men."

The 1940 show included a demonstration by the anti-tank corps from Shilo, and a mock bombing-run in front of the grandstand, with a sack of flour being substituted for the real thing.

The grandstand show adopted the war theme. The 1941 production "Music on Wings" ended with a passionate rendition of "There'll Always be an England." The next year, Gitz Rice, a member of the famous Dumb-Bells revue of World War I, was the headline attraction on a roster which included Flight Sergeant Mahoney—alias Fifi the Clown—supplied by the Royal Canadian Air Force.

Signs of the war permeated all parts of the fair. Advertising posters no longer contained the prominent buffalo logo of the pre-war period, for that animal had been dropped in favour of a presentation featuring a sailor, airman, and soldier. Victory Loan drives were well promoted during the fair, and the exhibition grounds were turned over to the bond drive organizers for special events. In the 1942 exhibition, prizes were offered for a Victory Farm Flock (Sheep) event to replace the previous year's Victory Wool contest. That fair also included Victory Hog and Victory Hen contests. Two years later, a war-time canning class was added to the schedule. In keeping with war-time rationing regulations, competitors were not permitted to use sugar.

The Provincial Exhibition also seized on the war to help their advance ticket sale campaigns. The attempt to sell tickets through the mail had run into government opposition in the late 1930s, but the experience had demonstrated a broad interest in such contests. The 1941 contest involved a "Win-the-War" quiz which invited contestants to return their answers to the fair. The event was widely promoted; some $800 was spent on advertising in the United States alone. It obviously worked, for over 35,000 entries were returned. The contest earned a handsome profit, but the directors were not convinced that the heavy promotion was appropriate during the war. The next year, a "Hunt the Spy" contest, held without much promotion, ran into difficulties when contestants complained about the non-payment of prizes. The event was continued in 1943, but although a small profit was again realized, it was decided to cancel future contests.

The attempts to highlight the war reflected the directors' desire to demonstrate their commitment to assist the war effort

1940 6 December
When directors were challenged over their refusal to give their insurance business to the low bidder on a tender call, N.W. Kerr defended board practice, stating that the insurance committee thought it advisable to give the largest portion of the insurance coverage to directors who were in the business because of their contribution to the board.

1942 23 June

At the meeting of exhibition directors a letter was read from the Royal Canadian Air Force stating that Flight Sergeant Mahoney would be placed on loan for the summer fair. Sgt. Mahoney was soon to be better known to exhibition audiences by his professional name, "Fifi the Clown."

87　*Nothing was ever too garish or bizarre for a sideshow banner.*

88　*An "attraction"? of the 1941 exhibition.*

Some argued that operating the fair during a time of intense national crisis was inappropriate, but the board remained convinced that the encouragement of agriculture and the entertainment they provided justified their efforts. They also worried that it would be hard to re-establish the summer show after a few years' break.

Still, the national war effort understandably interfered with the smooth functioning of the annual event. The transportation priorities of the federal government did not always mesh with those of the exhibition, and the fair-goers, exhibitors and carnival operators had to make adjustments. The war also cut into the annual grants for exhibition prize lists, already suffering from the frequent reductions made during the Depression days. Gasoline rationing limited the ability of fair-goers to reach the grounds, special train rates for competitors were cancelled and a shortage of men of military age made it difficult to find suitable help. In 1942, the Wartime Prices and Trades Board prohibited the display of farm machinery at the exhibition for the duration. The directors mourned the loss of this major fair attraction, but since government regulations strictly controlled the distribution of such machinery these commercial displays were obviously redundant. Such alterations, and in particular the farmers' difficulties in securing adequate labor, even forced a reduction in the length of the livestock show. A number of directors, led by staunch traditionalist N.W. Kerr, protested the change but it went ahead regardless. Kerr's warning that the shift from the five-day to a three-day livestock show would "ruin the Fair entirely" proved incorrect.

89 *W.A. Cameron, exhibition president, 1941-42.*

SOMEWHAT SURPRISINGLY, these changes did not lead to a decline in entries. Each year, the directors noted with pride that the agricultural entries steadily increased, despite a poor midway, travel difficulties, and prize reductions. It was a measure of the Brandon fair's status among Canadian exhibitions, and the fact that it was

117

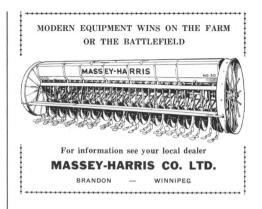

Come on, Canada

PRODUCE
FOR
VICTORY

**MANITOBA
WINTER FAIR**

Brandon, Manitoba

MARCH 16 - 17 - 18
1943

90 *Equipment dealers com-
pared the farm to the battle-
field. From the 1942 winter
fair program.*

91 *During the war, farmers
were urged to "produce for
victory." This theme is por-
trayed in the exhibition
program of 1943.*

one of the few able to operate a virtually standard show in the
midst of the war, that agricultural exhibitors maintained and even
expanded their participation.

While livestock entries were rising, it seemed as though war-
time conditions would end harness racing at the fair. The 1940
event lost money, prompting several directors to call for its abolition.
One director, W.L. McGregor, called for patience, and warned
against being too money-conscious. He drew attention "to the great
number of people who throng along the Track Ring—people who
are greatly interested in the races and have come many miles to
see them and yet cannot afford to purchase Grandstand Seats."
His defence carried the day, but the problem soon got worse. A
combination of gasoline rationing and Canadian regulations
threatened in 1941 to keep American horses at home. Races
scheduled for Deloraine, Carman and Portage were about to be
cancelled, although the Provincial Exhibition declared its intention
to continue. The immediate problem was resolved, but opponents
of racing within the organization kept up their pressure.

A move to drop racing entirely in 1942 almost succeeded,
but a compromise resulted in only a single day of harness racing
for the 1943 fair. The move had unexpected benefits. Racing fans
filled the stands for the event, generating what one director called
"the best afternoon grandstand receipts ever received on an
afternoon in the history of the Brandon Exhibition." Racing
appeared to have been saved. A two-day meet was held in 1944
and a move to increase the harness racing meet to three days in
1945 almost succeeded.

Although the balance sheet and attendance figures remained
favorable throughout the war, the Provincial Exhibition was not
the same as it had been before the war. The 1943 summer fair
was typical of the modest undertaking scheduled during this period.
War-time restrictions had limited the Conklin shows to only eight
rail cars. Unlike earlier years, when the forthcoming exhibition
attracted tremendous attention, the 1943 show had trouble

generating headlines in competition with front page stories of a Chinese advance on the Japanese, the German retreat on the eastern front and Allied bombing of Germany.

The fair management tried to address this problem by giving their show a war-time flavor. Visitors to the grounds found ample evidence of the war. The directors had hoped for a huge military extravaganza on the grounds in 1943 and asked the Department of National Defence to provide the manpower and equipment. That idea, which was also a thinly veiled attempt to circumvent travel restrictions on midway supplies, was vetoed, but four military bands and a few small army displays provided partial compensation. The grandstand show was appropriately entitled "Allies Victorious" and promised a patriotic revue of dancers, jugglers, singers and animal acts.

The Honorable D.L. Campbell, Minister of Agriculture, opened the fair with a declaration of the importance of continuing the exhibition during the war. The *Brandon Sun* recorded that he said:

> The contribution that livestock and agriculture makes in peace time is heightened in a period of war, because food must be furnished the fighting men. Because these factors are so vital to the successful prosecution of the war, I am glad to see the provincial exhibition carrying on.

The fair had indeed carried on, but without the trappings that had attracted so much attention in years past.

The 1943 fair did not have the usual collection of special events and attractions. Fair-goers who had visited the much-abbreviated midway, could wander through the elaborate school display or visit the extensive exhibit on modern food production hosted by the federal department of agriculture. Under the grandstand, an impressive flower show, entries of homecooking and "domestic manufacturing" were on display. There were only a few commercial exhibits, and many of them were primarily declarations of corporate patriotism. The T. Eaton Company display

92   *The Souris Clothing Club, in 1943 and again in 1944 won the T. Eaton trophy for their display.*

93   *Wm. Davidson, exhibition president, 1943-46.*

120

illustrated the battle fields of North Africa. Manitoba Hydro offered a more practical exhibit: the uses of electricity in modern homes.

Visitors to the 1943 exhibition might have been a bit disappointed if they had attended fairs before the war. The fair was the best that conditions would allow and, given the circumstances, was surprisingly good. When the war was over, the Provincial Exhibition would face a rather substantial challenge in bringing the summer fair back to the earlier status.

IF THE WAR YEARS HAD BEEN TOUGH for the summer exhibition, the directors nonetheless had little basis for complaint. The government had not requested all of their exhibition buildings and had paid a reasonable rent for those buildings it used. Military occupation was not really an impediment to the operations, a condition rather unique among western Canada's major exhibitions. The directors did not have to look very far to see the impact of an unfavorable government decision, for the Manitoba Winter Fair would not pass through the war unscathed.

Early in the war, the Department of National Defence approached the Brandon Winter Fair and Livestock Association, the holding company responsible for the winter fair buildings, to request the use of the arena and pavilion as a manning depot. The buildings were badly in need of repair, and the military authorities offered to undertake renovations in lieu of rent. An agreement was eventually struck in May 1940.

The Manitoba Winter Fair was now homeless. Still reeling from the financial problems left over after the Depression, the board was not in a strong position. The directors were nonetheless determined to carry on, as far as their limited means would allow. The Provincial Exhibition offered the use of its facilities for the winter fair, a less than perfect solution in that the buildings were not properly insulated. The army cooperated as much as possible, vacating the barns and stables it occupied during fair time.

The 1941 Winter Fair went ahead as scheduled, with the Provincial Exhibition providing their grounds and equipment free of charge. It was a generous offer, and typical of the long-standing cooperation between the two associations, but it did not prevent the show from being a financial disaster. Bills piled up year after year, the directors pressing on in hopes that their assistance to agriculture would be appreciated; and that they could prop up their show until they regained control of their buildings.

The directors did more than simply mark time. They scheduled special contests in an effort to boost attendance, picking such war themes as "Names in the War News" to highlight their commitment to the war effort. In 1941, they contemplated adding a small carnival to the proceedings in an attempt to broaden the appeal of their much reduced agricultural show, but decided they could not afford such expenses. The efforts did not work to any great extent. The livestock breeders and farmers continued to come, though in reduced numbers, but the city folks found little of interest in agricultural competitions held in inadequate facilities.

If one element characterized the activities of the winter fair board during the war years, it was the obvious commitment to agriculture. This had always been an agricultural show, more so than the summer fair, and the promotion of excellence in breeding and farming had been its principal aim. The loss of the arena and stables during the war obviously undercut this ability to maintain existing programs, but the directors persisted. When need warranted, special cattle and horse sales were held, again at the Provincial Exhibition grounds. The annual fall horse show was continued until 1943, when it was cancelled at the request of the Manitoba Clydesdale Horse Breeders' Club, who claimed not enough competitors could afford the time or money necessary to compete. Sheep and swine sales and competitions were held in conjunction with the fall show, while poultry joined cattle as the mainstays of the spring fair. The winter fair was unable to continue its main show on the scale of previous years, but the addition of these specialty events provided a useful service to the agricultural community.

The 1943 winter fair provides a particularly striking example of the modest expectations and continuing problems faced by the directors. Organizers had planned for a limited presentation, consisting of cattle judging, poultry events, swine competitions, and a large boys' and girls' competition. In addition, they planned a special education evening, consisting of addresses by a number of prominent western Canadian agriculturalists. The directors put together a reasonable program designed to further agricultural development, even if it all but ignored events of urban interest.

But before the modest fair began, disaster struck. A fierce March storm held the region firmly in its grip for several days. Exhibitors were caught either on their farms or en route. Speakers were unable to reach Brandon on time. The schedule was hastily revised. Judging events were postponed to give storm-stayed exhibitors time to reach the grounds. The educational program, initially slated for Monday evening was moved to Thursday then scrapped entirely when several of the keynote speakers were forced to cancel. Judging went ahead for those animals already in stable and animals available for sale found a reduced number of bidders.

The directors realized the extent of the debacle. Revenues had fallen some 40%, yet another savage blow to the already vulnerable organization. In true exhibition fashion, they declared their intention to carry on, even as they surveyed the storm damage. Continuing the fair proved difficult after 1943, as the association's bank accounts dipped perilously low. It was, however, characteristic of the association's steadfast intention to provide direct service to the agricultural sector through judging events, livestock sales and educational programs. Lack of money prevented them from doing much else.

The combination of a decade of Depression and the loss of the buildings during the war brought the Manitoba Winter Fair to the verge of financial ruin. The impending collapse of the winter fair generated a variety of responses. The holding company responsible for the building approached the provincial government in 1944, asking for the use of buildings at the Carberry Air Field. This eventually proved unnecessary, for soon after the Royal Canadian Air Force returned the Wheat City Arena. This did not solve the crisis with the winter fair, however, for both the holding company and the fair association were perilously close to bankruptcy.

THE PROBLEMS ENCOUNTERED by the holding company precipitated a major debate over the future of the two Brandon fairs and the associated buildings. The Brandon Winter Fair Association had had trouble paying its bills for a number of years, and the loss of revenue associated with the military take-over during World War II only added to its burdens. The financial distress of the Manitoba Winter Fair made matters worse, for both the holding company and the Provincial Exhibition were forced to write off debts the winter fair association could not pay. At one point early in 1941, the Provincial Exhibition even considered applying to the Manitoba government to have the winter fair buildings turned over to their organization.

The debate heated up by 1944. The military was about to turn the buildings back to the holding company, but that organization owed some $330,000 to the provincial government, a sum it had no hope of repaying. Since the buildings required extensive renovations before they could be used again for a fair, the problems seemed even greater. The logical solution to several directors of the Provincial Exhibition was to have the two boards amalgamate, with the new organization to be responsible for the facilities and financing of both the summer and winter fairs. That proposal carried its own set of risks, for the larger board would have extremely heavy financial obligations. After considering the risks, the Provincial Exhibition dropped the idea.

FOOD for FREEDOM

MANITOBA WINTER FAIR

BRANDON, MANITOBA

MARCH 15, 16, and 17
1944

CANADA
POSTAGE PAID
3 C.
Permit No. 205

94 *Both the winter fair and the summer exhibition supported Canada's war effort in many ways. This is the cover of the winter fair program, 1944.*

95   *A feed dealer selling for victory.*

96   *Equipment dealers had to face wartime restrictions as well. This advertisement in the 1944 winter fair program reflects their concern.*

97   *Bank promotion in the 1944 exhibition program.*

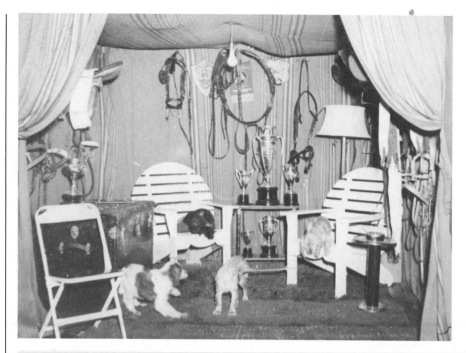

98   *Macpherson's tack room at the 1945 winter fair.*

99   *George and Jimmy MacArthur and a six-horse team belonging to MacArthur and Sons, 1945.*

126

❧ *1946 21 February*
At their regular meeting the winter fair directors debated and approved a motion that the $95,000 worth of fire insurance, "be divided equally between the seven insurance agents who are shareholders of this Association."

100 *The midway at night —victory over the dark years of war.*

This left the problem with the Brandon Winter Fair Association (the holding company), the Manitoba Winter Fair, the City of Brandon and the provincial government. Declaring that "the Manitoba Winter Fair cannot hope to continue such restricted operation indefinitely nor can it serve the public interest as it should because of lack of revenue," the latter association petitioned the Manitoba government to turn ownership of the buildings over to the City of Brandon. The province agreed, favoring "a continuing responsible body representing all of the citizens of Brandon" over the other option of granting the buildings to the Provincial Exhibition. The government cleared all encumbrances, including the $200,000 mortgage it held plus the $140,000 in unpaid interest, and passed the buildings on to the city government in December 1945. The final agreement called for the City of Brandon to operate and maintain the winter fair buildings, although it was obliged to turn the facilities back over to the Manitoba Winter Fair for one week each fall for the fall sales and for three weeks surrounding the annual event. By the fall of 1946, the old holding company, the Brandon Winter Fair and Livestock Association had ceased operations.

It had appeared for a time that the debate over the winter fair building would precipitate the long-promoted merger of the two Brandon fairs. While the formal merger remained elusive, the two associations worked closely together. They had cooperated extensively through the depression and the war years, and the richer Provincial Exhibition of Manitoba had provided several loans to keep the winter fair solvent.

As before, the two exhibitions continued to share a secretary-manager. J.E. Rettie, with the organization since the fall of 1923, resigned in September 1940, largely because the cancellation of the winter fair and the contraction of the summer show had significantly reduced his work load. Beatrice Benson, who had been with the exhibitions for a number of years as an office assistant was hired, at a reduced salary, to replace him. Continuing a tradition first started by W. I. Smale, Benson served as the secretary for a number of breed associations, with the provision that she turn her salary from these duties over to the fairs. Miss Benson remained with the fairs until September 1945. She was replaced for a time by Alice Hogeland, who held the post while a search was conducted for a permanent replacement. In December 1945, the Provincial Exhibition hired S.C. McLennan of New Westminster, British Columbia. McLennan had been the manager of the exhibition in Vancouver, before he quit over a policy dispute. The hiring of McLennan, a professional fair manager with excellent prairie contacts and a solid reputation, was a suitable start to a new era.

As the gloom of war slowly lifted, the exhibition associations prepared themselves for an uncertain future. No one was sure that the economic distress of the Depression would not return. The demobilization of the soldiers after World War I had brought unemployment, labor unrest and general protest. Canadians justifiably wondered if this experience would be repeated once more. That, however, was a matter for next year. In 1945, it was time to celebrate the end of the war, to remember the personal and collective sacrifices, and to reflect on what Canada had accomplished. For Brandon's exhibitions, it was time to repair the financial damage, fix the neglected buildings and prepare for life in the post-war world.

In that last quarter-hour before showtime there is a friendly murmur of anticipation from the slowly-gathering crowd. Friends greet friends and scan the swelling audience for neighbors. In the orchestra pit, musicians don their dark jackets and arrange their music. In the infield behind the garish sets there is increasing activity as performers practice their juggling and make exits and entrances from their little cluster of parked trailers. Sharp at eight the conductor raps his baton on the music stand. The opening fanfare pours out through the sound system and reverberates through the grandstand. The master of ceremonies enters from stage left and the magic begins.

The old grandstand shows are history now. Through years of television—color and close-ups and instant replays—we have 'attended' the world's fantastic events, from royal weddings to moon walks, from grand opera to screaming rock concerts. And yet, the fuzzy warm memories remain.

For old times' sake, let me take you back—backstage for many of those fondly remembered grandstand shows....

First, the master of ceremonies. He was an integral part of the show who did much more than simply introduce the acts. He, and invariably this was a male's position, was announcer, straight man, and practicing crowd psychologist. At the top of the show, his assignment was to give an elaborate introduction. For this there was an unbreakable tradition, his flow of adjectives, and adjectival phrases.

We were told who the impresario was, and usually this was Fred Kressman, or Ernie Young, and there was a long period at Brandon in which these men alternated as producer of the "night show." The emcee then gave us the theme, which usually had one foot in ethnic history and the other in some global undertaking.

This done, however, it still was not time for the opening act; the master of ceremonies had to give his inventory of adjectives their annual work-out, which he did with a catalogue of acts and performers. This year's parade of talent was 'unsurpassed'. The aerial acts were 'death-defying'. The animal acts were quite clearly 'world-renowned'. The soprano and the baritone had sung command performances before the 'crowned heads of Europe'.

One day in Chicago, at a luncheon during the annual meeting of the Showman's League of America, I challenged Fred Kressman on this subject, taking the position that this standard format was over the hill, heavy with years.

He laughed. As I was to learn, this man was a shrewd reader of crowds, and this was as it had to be, for his income depended upon his ability to satisfy the entertainment needs of those who patronized agricultural fairs.

"Friend," he said with a sigh, as if he were reluctant to give me the lecture I was going to get, "you've lived on the Canadian prairies for so long that you don't know your own people; you *can't* know them objectively, you're one of them. Those of us who sell acts on the Class "A" circuit call your people a 'red bloomer' crowd."

Fred could see the question forming in my mind so he answered it before it was asked.

"A 'red bloomer' crowd is a farm audience. Once each night they want to see the clown do something which causes his suspenders to break and his baggy pants to fall down. You'll remember last year this happened while he was hanging from the high wire. Well, when this happens the audience learns that he's wearing women's knickers, that they're grossly over-sized, and always, always bright red. Last year, when I gave you 'Carnival of Nations,' those bloomers gave you the biggest laugh of the evening... and it worked *every* evening from Brandon right through to Port Arthur and Fort William six weeks later. Your crowd likes things done the same way every year. My job is to give them what they want."

Let me not forget that clown or those bloomers, for the clown was a key part of the show. He provided the comic relief which was mixed in with music, human talent, animal talent, balance, surprises, apprehension, smiles, and thrills which allegedly defied death.

The headline act was as functional as the heading in your newspaper; its duty was to attract attention. It was the second highest paid act, second only to the one which closed the show. The opener set the pace, set the theme, elevated public expectations that, for the next two hours, there would be exposed before them their entire annual intake of professional entertainment. Farmers, folks from the small towns, city residents, wives and mothers and over-tired kids gathered nightly in batches of 5000 for the annual 'extravaganza'.

Those few experts in the crowd could tell you the format of the night show even before the conductor's baton was raised. We—yes, I include myself— knew that there would be two high spots, the opening and the closing. We knew as well that in between there was a collection of fillers, many parts of which were inter-changeable, for showfolk are endlessly adaptable. Someone from the juggling act could throw knives, or imitate birdcalls, or perform some magic if the impresario needed to stretch things out for another ten minutes. If there had to be a cover-up because some mechanical apparatus was being erected, the emcee would engage in banter with the clown, usually of the 'red bloomer' variety.

Each year, when the first performance kicked off another week of night shows, there were two or three of us who'd previously seen most of the acts. We were members of the exhibition's attractions committee. It was part of our duty to visit Chicago in December during the annual meeting of the Showmen's League of America. Each evening there was a banquet which was followed by a parade of talent, performers whom their promoters viewed as ready to venture out onto the fair and exhibition circuit.

Only once each year would this audience be gathered in one hall. Included were directors from all the fairs in North America. In the wings were persons who referred to themselves as 'impresarios', but were known to the trade as 'flesh pedlars'. They were the booking agents who would provide work for the entertainers. If Fred Kressman, say,

or Ernie Young could assemble a two-hour show for $10,000 a week, then he would set about finding bookings for which he might be paid twice that amount.

Over the many years of the "A" circuit on the Prairies, an elaborate means of selection evolved. Late on the morning of the last day of the showmen's convention, we members of all the attractions committees on the circuit gathered in a committee room in the Hotel Sherman. The chairman duly cautioned us that no one could leave the room until the final votes were counted. Luncheon was served inside. If someone had to go to the restroom, an attendant went along so that no surreptitious telephone call could be made to tip one producer onto what his opposition was offering.

Those impresarios bidding for the six-week circuit, the "A" circuit plus the Lakehead show, drew lots to make their presentations before the committee. One after another they outlined their theme, explained its significance, then began the detailed pedigrees of those acts they held under contract. I can recall the whole lot of us writing feverishly as we listed the names of jugglers, acrobalancers, vocalists, and high-wire performers. We soon learned to place heavy discounts on words like 'smash', 'boffo', 'socko', and phrases like 'show-stopper'."

For the uninitiated, Showmen's League meetings were a learning experience, and one of the important lessons was that there is a complete society under the generic name of 'show business'.

For these, the Chicago convention was a command performance. I note in

my diary for 1952 that, on successive nights at our banquet table, I visited with lawyers who specialized in show business, with bankers who financed the major operators, with suppliers whose entire livelihood was involved with the world of outdoor entertainment. I met Bernie Mendelssohn, whose company made tents or 'tops', as he called them. Ida Cohen operated a sizeable insurance brokerage which covered shows and performers. I still have the card of Ned Furtillo, which tells me that he is a salesman for 'gaming equipment'. His biggest line was stuffed toys used for prizes.

Life is rough in show business. One evening when the banquet was over I went up in the elevator with a man I'd met earlier at the Brandon show. His name was Kinky Wolfe, and he was a jewellery salesman. He made his money from the fact that people in show business like to be turned out in the flashiest manner possible. Harry Julius often told me stories about his fellow showfolk. He said it was the mark of a true 'carnie', that if he were down to his last $1.75, he wouldn't save it for food; instead he'd go out and get a manicure, the better he'd look when he went to put the touch on someone.

Kinky knew all this, and explained it to me one day at lunch at the Prince Edward. He told me that many of his regular customers, with holes in their soles, and no certainty of the next meal, would flash a quarter-carat diamond ring, or a diamond-studded Shrine lapel badge.

Remember Gus Yaeger? He used to wear a fur coat on the Brandon midway on the hottest days in July; this was his means of having his merchandise with him as he visited the carnival people. He measured showmen's wives for coats during the Brandon show and delivered them five weeks later in Regina.

Kinky also had a mobile showroom. He had his suitcoat fitted up on the inside with innumerable tiny pockets. In a conversation with a possible 'mark', he'd open his coat, and within a matter of seconds he would be displaying necklaces, watches, rings, even uncut gems for the big winner who wanted to smuggle an investment back to the states.

On the night I went up in the elevator with Kinky, we said farewell at my door, and he continued down the hallway. I went to bed; friend Kinky went to hospital. Waiting for him inside his room were two thugs who beat him unconscious and made off with the contents of his coat-of-many-pockets. Estimated value: $38,000.

The grandstand show was a creature of the night, the darker the night the better. Only when the lighting could be controlled was the night show at its best. I once viewed it as a waste of time when we felt we had to run grandstand matinees for the kids. Members of that audience faced north and within their view was a vast panorama: a tiny stage on the verge of a racetrack, an infield filled with trucks and trailers, a long row of racehorse stables, a rail line, the skyline of the city. A juggler or a balancing act had to be good indeed to capture attention in such a setting.

Even in the evening, when that long, slow, colorful prairie sunset is at its most spectacular, the first half of the show often failed to capture the public's attention. In this period the lighting was simply ineffective, the stage settings subdued; even the sequins had no sparkle.

Only in total darkness could the night show live up to its name and become a grand stand. Only in the out-of-doors blackness could show business display its magic, the ability to transport you and your imagination into a czar's court, or a fairy kingdom. In those happy days of the early fifties, we had such a demand for tickets that we staged two complete performances every Thursday and Friday.

In the thirties, and forties, and for almost exactly half of the fifties, Prairie audiences appreciated the grandstand show for what it was, a means of transporting us into a different galaxy. For two hours every year patrons forgot about manure forks, mortgage payments, and those other exigencies of farmstead and homestead.

For this brief period each year we were quite honestly spellbound as act followed act. Right on cue we gasped, chuckled, sucked in our collective breath, and roared out those belly laughs. It was even possible for some of us over the years to trace connections between one aspect of show business and another. One evening as I sat with 5000 others and watched a slender teen-ager fired from a cannon by her father, Alfredo Zucchini, I would never have guessed that in ten years she would be back on the "A" circuit in another capacity, the brand-new bride of Carl Sedlmayr, Jr.

Even more unlikely was the connection between television and the grandstand show. I saw my first TV in the Sedlmayr suite at the Hotel Sherman in,

I think, 1952. Harry Julius used another miraculous invention, a Polaroid camera, to photograph me in front of that set, a picture still in my exhibition clipping file. Never could I have reckoned at that time that this great leap in electronic communication would sound the death knell of our connection with outdoor showbiz. The availability of entertainment in the livingroom all day every day spelled the end of these delightful open-air, summertime presentations. In retrospect, it is surprising to think that those early shows, encompassing no more than two hours every year, still fill such a prominent spot in the memories of we old exhibition fans.

Fred McGuinness

Chapter Four

1946-1960

Years of Renewal

1946 2 July

"The fair grounds are plentifully provided with lunch rooms, hot dog stands and refreshment booths, in most cases carried on by commercial firms. Local organizations are also busy this week serving the public by providing meals and lunches. First Church United Ladies Aid has a counter in the southwest corner of the display building and serves hot meals as well as lunches. The W.A. of the First Baptist Church has a lunchroom and refreshment counter at the east end of the grandstand."
from the *Brandon Sun*.

1946 6 September

"The manager reported that 110 prisoners of war camped in tents on our grounds and are using the Fire Hall as a cook house. The Department of Labor has agreed to pay us $100.00 for this privilege; water and light bills are to be paid by them."
from the P.E.M. minutes.

101   *An aerial view of the exhibition grounds, c.1950.*

In 1946, THE DIRECTORS OF BRANDON'S FAIRS looked back on the previous decade and a half with some wonderment. They had piloted their associations through some very difficult times. With the war finally behind them, the Provincial Exhibition of Manitoba and the Manitoba Winter Fair could get back to business. It would take a few years to re-establish the shows to their former stature, to convince the farm folks that the summer and winter shows still deserved a prominent place in their annual schedule, to prove to the citizens of Brandon that the combination of education, agricultural and entertainment really provided something for everyone, and to demonstrate to civic boosters that the fairs offered an unparalleled means for the promotion of their city.

Post-war conditions differed significantly from earlier periods. Canadians left the war uncertain about what lay ahead, concerned in particular that the Depression of the 1930s would soon descend again on the country. It took time to transform that caution into confidence. The federal government helped, demonstrating a commitment to employment and providing social services that had been sorely missing during the depression. Continued government spending and the release of pent-up consumer demand held in check by more than six years of strict government rationing and military production priorities eased the transition from the war-time economy to the greater prosperity of the 1950s.

The transition was not rapid, and signs of the military commitments of the past faded slowly. Brandon had been surrounded by army camps and the flying schools of the Commonwealth Air Training Program. Demobilization occurred gradually, deliberately scheduled by the government in an attempt to prevent the hasty release of ex-service personnel that had caused such chaos after World War I. But the rural Manitoba camps were eventually closed, leaving only the army's Camp Shilo and the Royal Canadian Air Force base at Rivers.

Two of these military establishments had been located on exhibition property. The Wheat City Arena, home of the winter fair, had been taken over by the air force in 1940 and returned to the holding company, the Brandon Winter Fair and Livestock Association, in 1944. That had not immediately solved the lingering financial problems of the B.W.F.L.A. and its major tenant, the Manitoba Winter Fair. Neither organization had the money to operate or renovate the facility and so the buildings were turned over to the Manitoba government. The Provincial Exhibition had attempted to assume control of the assets of the B.W.F.L.A., but that effort was thwarted by the provincial government, which passed on control of the buildings to the City of Brandon.

This attempt to expand their holdings was not the only problem involving property which faced the Provincial Exhibition. During the war, the army had built a camp, known as "A-4," on exhibition property south of the Normal School. With the advent of peace, President William Davidson and two of his directors, Judge A.G. Buckingham and the redoubtable N.W. Kerr, took the position that the A-4 buildings were now the property of the exhibition and laid plans to develop them for future exhibition purposes. In the midst of their own preparations, they learned that the City of Brandon was negotiating with the War Assets Corporation to purchase the same structures. The troubled relationship between the city and the exhibition was further clouded by the fact that the city had commandeered some exhibition buildings during the war for commercial purposes. They continued to collect rents which the directors felt should be turned over to them. Nor could the directors forget the one remaining legacy of their war-time participation; there were still 100 German prisoners-of-war living in tents in Exhibition Park.

While Kerr and Buckingham continued their negotiations with the City of Brandon on the tangled legacy left over from the war, other board members turned their attentions to the future. First signs looked extremely promising. In 1946 the exhibition directors increased the prize money for cattle and poultry classes by 25%, and for other classes by 10%, a sure sign of financial

102 *Judge A. Gordon Buckingham. Both as a lawyer and later as a jurist he served on the exhibition board; president 1947-48.*

135

103 *Machinery row in the early fifties, viewed from the top of the grandstand.*

104 *The six-horse team judging class in the outdoor show ring, summer fair, c.1951.*

136

stability and confidence. It was a well-timed move, for the balance sheet that year showed a profit of almost $10,000. Prosperity put expansion back on the association's agenda. There were a number of suggestions, including renovations to many existing buildings, the addition of 12 rows of seats to the main grandstand and an extension of the smaller livestock grandstand. A number of minor renovations were actually carried out, although the more grandiose plans discussed in the directors' fanciful moments would have to wait for a much later date.

The post-war years proved kind for the Provincial Exhibition. An expansion of the grandstand show, the extremely popular midway of Royal American Shows, and a variety of agricultural, commercial and entertainment exhibits combined to make the Brandon summer fair a crowd favorite. For the directors, this was not a time to tinker with success. The modifications to the existing schedule were modest, primarily changes of scale rather than substance, and with good reason, for the fair audience was obviously pleased with the annual show.

THE EXHIBITION'S COMMITMENT TO AGRICULTURE remained very much in evidence, although the management was forced to admit repeatedly that most of the fair-goers came for entertainment, not cattle shows and poultry competitions. A special effort was made to keep young people involved. In 1947, for example, more than 1,000 boys and girls attended the annual farm camps, a number that would double within a decade; the directors felt this participation of western Canada's future farmers represented "excellent publicity." The annual 4-H show became a prime agriculture feature, drawing hundreds of exhibitors each year. The exhibition had to appeal to the Department of National Defence on several occasions for the loan of additional cots when enrolment exceeded expectations. In 1957, for example, more than 130 4-H members entered their animals in the beef competition.

The Provincial Exhibition also added a calf scramble as a special event for junior farmers. The procedure was simple. Ten calves were introduced at one end of the show ring, and 20 teenagers at the other. Those fortunate enough to put their halter on one of the calves got to take the animal home, although they were expected to enter it in the judging competitions the following year. The feature proved extremely popular, both among the young participants and the audience. It was less popular with the Manitoba Department of Agriculture, which did not see it appropriate to hold such entertainment events in conjunction with the 4-H gathering. The exhibition in 1957 entered into a long-term arrangement with Labatt's Brewery for sponsorship of the event, which further lessened offical interest in the calf scramble. The department still felt it necessary to underline its position that neither scrambling for calves nor association with a brewery was in any way acceptable to the 4-H movement.

The Provincial Exhibition always attempted to maintain a healthy friendship with federal and provincial officals, who provided consistent support for the exhibition's agricultural program, and were often the strongest defenders of the exhibition in the constant turmoil of budgetary debates. The loyalty of the government officials was essential, as the agricultural programs were far from self-supporting. Although profits generated from gate receipts, the midway, and special attractions helped to subsidize the money-losing judging events, government grants were essential to the continuation of a well-funded prize list.

The Provincial Exhibition had always been well-supported in this regard, largely because of its lofty status as the premier agricultural event in the province. Ottawa had for many years provided capital grants for approved projects, usually exhibit buildings, and generous prize-list money for specific livestock classes. Provincial assistance had also been forthcoming for both physical improvements and subsidies for the agricultural events.

The summer fair had also been the benificiary of financial

105   *The first calf scramble, winter fair, 1957.*

106   *For many years the displays of new automobiles were a feature of the summer exhibition. At one time they occupied an entire building. This picture shows a couple inspecting a 1950 Monarch.*

139

107 *The Manitoba Government Building was erected in 1927 as a centre in which provincial departments could explain their functions and services to exhibition patrons. In later years it was used for school exhibits, and in 1952 was adapted for use as the Trade Show Building.*

THE MANITOBA
TRADE FAIR

support from the City of Brandon. That aid had been in evidence since the first stallion sale in the 1880s, although political tensions and different priorities occasionally tarnished the relationship. In 1929 and again in 1948, the city had agreed to underwrite debenture issues, and this support had evolved over time into an annual civic grant of $8,600. The money was not always forthcoming. In 1951, for example, the payment was deferred because of heavy civic expenditures in "more important" areas. The exhibition board nonetheless came to rely on this support, an expression of continued civic interest in the fair. The exisiting arrangement was subject to periodic renewal, and was to be reviewed in 1958, although there was little indication that citizens of Brandon would alter this friendly relationship.

SUCH SEEMINGLY MUNDANE MATTERS seldom detracted the exhibition directors from their principal work. Their main task was to maintain the affection and support of urban and rural fair-goers. For the first decade of the post-war period, these efforts appeared to be succeeding gloriously. Attendance had never been higher. Year after year, thousands attended the annual show, drawn by Royal American Shows' stunning midway and carnival, the dramatic presentation of the nightly grandstand show, the commercial and government displays which jammed the exhibition buildings, and the agricultural competitions. The grandstand shows maintained their special status, as the presentations brought first-rate performers into a region poorly served by professional entertainers. Although on the surface there appeared to be little reason to tamper with the obvious success of the summer spectacular, the directors were aware of the need to keep their show current.

One sign of that change could be seen on the association's letterhead. Though the slogan "Show Window of Manitoba" maintained its place of pride, a new line, "Western Canada Trade Fair," was now in evidence across the top. The exhibition had long attempted to highlight the work of provincial and regional

108 *Brandon Packers, under the proprietorship of J.C. Donaldson, was one of the strongest commercial supporters of both summer and winter fairs. This is the company's display at the summer fair, c.1952.*

109 *One of the many local commercial displays at the summer fair, c.1953.*

141

manufacturers. Armed with substantial government support, the exhibition built a new exhibit hall for this show and, with the assistance of the Manitoba Department of Industry and Commerce, managed to fill it with commercial displays, most of them from Winnipeg. The exhibition tried to generate the maximum coverage from this event. A highlight of each summer fair was the annual Trade Fair Luncheon, well-attended by Winnipeg business leaders who drove to Brandon in motor cavalcades. Exhibition director Edson Boyd organized a special feature with Winnipeg's needle-trade promoters to stage fashion parades in the Trade Show Building, as well as in front of the grandstand during matinee performances.

Reading beyond the attendance figures, the exhibition directors had been searching for a new direction for their annual fair. A slow decline in fair revenues painted a far less rosy picture of the future than did the healthy crowds on the midway or in the grandstand. It seemed, for a time, as though the Trade Fair would provide that new direction. Director Judge A.G. Buckingham offered lavish praise of the national publicity the attraction was receiving; the 1953 presentation had been featured in the *Financial Post*. The growth of the show was further symbolized by the appointment of I.A. Toews in 1953 as an assistant manager with specific responsibility for trade fair business. Even as the Trade Show was building into a centerpiece of the summer fair, there were signs that the future was likely to be less bright than early signs had suggested. R.A. MacEachern, editor of the *Financial Post* had been recruited in 1956 to officiate at the opening ceremonies, and act as guest speaker at the annual luncheon, an apparent sign of the growing status of the feature. There were, however, distressing signs that the Trade Fair might be in trouble. Commercial display space rentals had dropped to 78 from 84 the previous year. It was a small percentage, perhaps, but to directors who had counted on the attraction to lead the exhibition into the 1960s, it was a most troubling sign.

110 *For many years the Kinsmen car raffle occupied a choice location on the midway immediately south of the grandstand. Shown here at the 1952 exhibition.*

The decline of the summer fair, although partially evident by the late 1950s, would not begin in earnest until the next decade. Between 1946 and 1958, annual changes and special features were kept to a minimum. With the co-operation of provincial kennel clubs, the exhibition in 1946 operated a four-day dog show. The following year, the special feature was a typewriting competition hosted by the Underwood Company. A few continuing features also were begun in this period. R.B. Alexander of the Brandon Kinsmen Club approached the directors in 1947 with the suggestion that a major car raffle be conducted each year in conjunction with the fair. The Kinsmen Club operated this annual feature, with the prize drawn during the grandstand show on the final evening; the exhibition received a share of the ticket sales in return for providing space and publicity. A decade later, in 1958, Western Manitoba Broadcasters, owners of CKX radio and television, contracted for a major exhibit in the Automobile Building. They promised to spend $2,000 on improvements to this under-used facility and to use the space for live radio and television broadcasts.

On an even larger scale, in 1955 a special "Dream Home" contest was held. Promoter R.A. Hodges approached the exhibition directors with his plans for a spectacular lottery. It seemed, on the surface, to be a fool-proof plan. Hodges and his two assistants undertook to sell booth space in the Trade Fair Building to companies which either sold or manufactured items of interest to home-owners. Those firms which contracted for space to display their paint, or appliances or television sets, also had to buy an advertisement in the exhibition program. Those programs were, in turn, sold on the grounds by Kinsmen and their wives at $1. The numbered programs gave the purchaser the chance to win the "Dream Home," a pre-fabricated house worth $12,000 and equipped with $8,000 worth of appliances and furniture which was on display on the grounds during fair week.

Several aspects of the promotion worked according to Hodges' plan. The furnished house was provided, the programs were printed, and the Brandon Kinsmen sold 15,088 tickets at $1 each. The winning ticket was drawn, and the home awarded to Mrs. Charles Saunderson of Souris. The exhibition did not, however, receive the $3,000 profit promised by the promoter. A month after the exhibition, S.A. Magnacca, president of the Brandon Builders Exchange, official "sponsors" of the feature, attended a meeting of the board to report that the "Dream Home" building accounts showed a shortage of $5,500.

The matter did not end there, although the exhibition directors were prepared to chalk up the losses to experience. Three years later, promoter R.A. Hodges sued the Edmonton fair, claiming that the fair had conspired to refuse him business, ostensibly because of the "Dream Home" debacle in 1955. He offered to withdraw his suit if he was paid $25,000. The other Class "A" exhibitions helped pay the award, but only after Hodges signed an agreement promising not to sue any other fairs. Brandon was responsible for $2,000. Although the directors would approach such "guaranteed" events with greater caution in the future, the fair-goers had obviously enjoyed the attraction, and the "Dream Home" event was tried again in 1956 and 1957.

ALTHOUGH THIS WAS AN ERA of little change in the summer fair, there were some important organizational changes. On 25 October 1953, the directors of both the summer and winter fairs were saddened to learn of the death of their secretary-manager S.C. McLennan. Although he had resided in the Wheat City for only eight years, he had become "one of Brandon's most esteemed citizens" in the opinion of the editors of the *Brandon Sun*. He had held the manager's position for eight years, and had provided positive and cheerful leadership that earned him plaudits from directors, exhibitors and government officials alike. The funeral of McLennan, at one-time commanding officer of the 26th Field Regiment, was conducted with full military honours and was

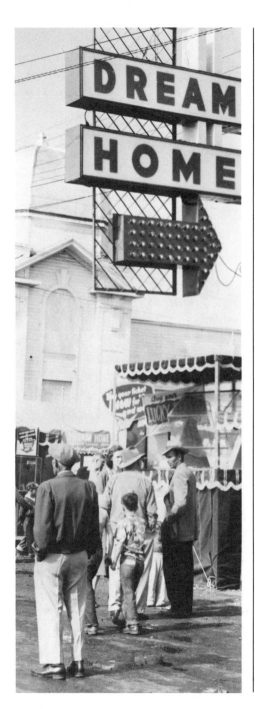

111   *A midway scene at the summer fair, 1955. The grandiose plans for the Dream Home did not work out precisely as the promoters had promised.*

112 *Exhibition board members on the grandstand for opening ceremonies, 1953.*
Front row:
Bob Macpherson, Roy Hopper, Harvey Tolton, Bob McClement, Bill Parker, Mayor James Creighton, Wilf McGregor, Frank Meighen, John Turner, Roy Clark, Roy Rice, Jim Moffatt, Bob Smith, Bill Boreskie.
Back row:
George Fitton, Dave Brown, Avery Harrison, Ted Higgens, Bill McGregor, M.J. Tinline, Wes Pentland, (unidentified), (unidentified), (unidentified), Tony Burneski, Alex McPhail, Bill Davidson.

attended by delegations from all the fairs on the Class "A" circuit.

Even as they mourned their loss, the directors had to turn their attentions toward finding a new manager. In December, a replacement was found within the exhibition association. Without informing the candidate in advance of his intentions, N.W. Kerr rose at the board meeting and nominated Peter Alexander McPhail as the new manager for a one-year term. The other directors applauded the wisdom of Kerr's suggestion and petitioned McPhail to accept. He was an excellent choice. McPhail was widely respected as an exhibitor, having shown his hogs, horses, and cattle nationally. He was a conspicious success as a farmer, and only recently had turned his farm over to his sons and moved to Brandon. He was a strong believer in agriculture as the backbone of the nation and farming as society's highest calling. His selection also re-established the tradition of appointing a manager from within the association, a pattern that would be adopted frequently in subsequent years.

Other changes in fair management proceeded more slowly. In the months leading up to the 1958 exhibition, a move was made to break the solid male hold on the directorate. Vice-President Harvey Tolton, in a suggestion characteristic of the pragmatism of the prairie farmer, felt that adding females to the board would solve a pressing problem. It was common practice at that time to hire staff to supervise such classes as homecraft, school art, and horticulture. To Tolton, the answer was to recruit female volunteers and give them semi-offical status. The proposition for a "board of lady directors" was debated. The issue was held in abeyance for a time when the manager advised the board that "only people representing organizations or associations were entitled to be associate members". That did not stop the association from establishing a Women's Advisory Committee, made up of Mrs. D. Elviss, Mrs. D. Graham, Mrs. G. McRae and Mrs. F. Heeney, to provide advice and assistance on specific aspects of the programme. The all-male bastion of the Provincial Exhibition board of directors would

113 *P.A. McPhail, exhibitor, director, general manager, president, and, over many years, the driving force for both winter and summer fairs.*

prove resilient, and it would be a few years yet before a woman finally found a place on the board.

As the board wrestled with internal problems, they remained wary of the ever-present threat posed to their fair by Winnipeg. The directors learned in 1955 that the federal entomological service was being removed from Brandon. Over many years both the summer and winter shows had enjoyed a close relationship with this office and its staff. The 'bug men' had been willing volunteer lecturers on the control of warble flies and grasshoppers and had often provided informational displays for the shows. Now the Brandon office was to be closed and its staff re-located in — of all places — Winnipeg. Board members sent a letter of protest to Ottawa which reminded federal officials that:

> "Brandon is the agricultural centre of Manitoba and we have one of the finest experimental farms in the country."

but its protests were to no avail.

By 1958, the challenge from Winnipeg had taken on more serious dimensions. Since World War I, the Brandon fair had easily faced down the challenges of all other Manitoba fairs. Its size and importance had ensured that the prize plums in the form of government grants, carnival contracts, commercial displays and grandstand shows came to the Provincial Exhibition. Winnipeg had tried on several occasions to put together an exhibition, but had failed to match Brandon's success. Now they faced the first major challenge in years. Early in 1958, the Western Canadian Association of Exhibitions (WCAE) informed the Brandon directors that promoters in the Manitoba capital wanted their Red River Exhibition, a primarily entertainment show started shortly after World War II, accepted into full membership.

Brandon objected vigorously, and on substantial grounds. The rules were explicit, in the opinion of the Wheat City directors, that such membership was restricted to those fairs which could meet Canada Department of Agriculture qualifications for Class "A" fairs. They took the hard position that if Winnipeg fell short in

114 *This handsome means of transport was a feature of the 1957 Travellers' Day Parade. Earl Carlisle, of Carroll, drives Monoplane and Sailor. The passengers are officers of the Brandon Council of Women, Mrs. P.A. McPhail, Mrs. Flora Cowan in the back seat; Mrs. Stuart Schultz, Mrs. W.A. Wood, in the front.*

115   *Ritchie Macpherson and Dick Painter checking the program in the announcers' stand, at the summer fair.*

116   *Unloading 4-H calves at the summer fair in the early fifties. Jim Sopp, in the truck, and Jim Smith are two leaders of the Carroll clubs. Carol Smith watches.*

this regard, which required a substantial prize list for agricultural competitions, it also lacked any entitlement for admission to the exclusive circle. Because it was one of the founding members of the WCAE, Brandon's objections carried considerable weight. The Red River Exhibition was granted only "associate" membership. Brandon had not been able to keep Winnipeg out entirely, but the directors found some solace in learning that the Winnipeg show would be admitted only on a provisional basis, and at a decidedly lower status. The emergence of a larger Winnipeg fair held some fearsome portents for the future, as Brandon's show would soon face competition for carnival shows and entertainment features. In the short term, the apparent victory over the Red River Exhibition had guaranteed the status of the Provincial Exhibition in Brandon.

WHILE THERE WAS LITTLE CHANGE in the summer fair's traditional formula, the Manitoba Winter Fair was considerably more innovative. Efforts were undertaken to secure a greater audience in an attempt to balance the books and allow for expansion. Unlike the steady-state summer fair, the winter fair faced several major challenges and responded with creativity and determination in an attempt to continue its agricultural show during a time of declining interest in purely farm pursuits.

Financial restraints continued. Even though the demand for hotel rooms during the 1946 fair was so strong that both Canadian National and Canadian Pacific were asked to "spot" Pullman cars at their depots during the winter fair, the directors lacked the resources to capitalize properly on that interest. Years later, exhibitor-turned-fair administrator George MacArthur recalled that an emergency meeting of the winter fair board in 1946 was informed that the bank account held less than $100. Despite the shortage, it was decided to push ahead with the fair, which was financed largely from money raised by passing the hat among the fair directors.

117   *The entry of MacArthur and Sons, summer fair, c.1948.*

118   *Pioneers at the "Ex". A popular feature for many years was the Pioneers' Building. Long-time residents of the area were invited to attend, have a visit and a cup of tea, and record brief biographical details in the log.*

Shown above are, left to right: W.G. Buckley, Brandon, Mrs. A. Mitchell, Beresford, A. Anderson, and P. Forsythe.

From one of the log books, now in the possession of Mrs. P.A. McPhail of Brandon, Mr. Buckley's history is related as follows: "born Bruce County 1871, came to Manitoba 1897 and farmed near Forrest. Attended the Brandon Fair first in 1898. In 1907 won 100 dollars in gold presented by B.C. Wallace for the best team at the Fair".

119   *R.M. Hopper, winter fair president, 1947-49.*

120   *Roy Clark, winter fair president, 1950-52.*

121   *The Rt. Hon. James G. Gardiner, minister of agriculture for Canada, arrives for the 1950 winter fair. With him is the president, Roy Clark.*

122 *Champion Suffolk ram, owned and shown by R.M. Smith, c. 1952.*

123 *The exhibition swine show. This competition was held in a building which during the winter months was used by the Brandon Curling Club. It was destroyed by fire 4 January 1956.*

154

The public had responded positively to the return of the winter fair to the Wheat City Arena in 1946. Although financial restraints limited the show to a three-day event, the attendance of more than 2,000 farmers for an afternoon bull show and a full crowd for the evening competitions provided evidence of public interest. A special matinee performance attracted 2,500 school children. The final horse show included a presentation to Mrs. N. W. Kerr, wife of the long-time fair director. Prior to her marriage, Mrs. Kerr was Miss Bea Benson, secretary-manager of both the summer and winter fairs during the war years. The special honour accorded Mrs. Kerr was a fitting tribute to a couple whose dedication to Brandon's fairs was unquestioned.

Special effort was made to secure greater government assistance. An emergency request by director and alderman James Kirkcaldy to Brandon city council in 1946 brought an immediate $500 grant with a promise of an additional $500 if needed. Manitoba's minister of agriculture, Hon. D.L. Campbell, promised to continue to subsidize one-third of the prize money. Appeals to the federal minister of agriculture in 1947 resulted in a one-time grant of $10,000 for repairs and improvements to the arena and a continuing $5,000 annual subsidy for the fair. The civic, provincial and federal assistance placed the winter fair on a more secure footing. When supplemented with prize list assistance from the breed associations, major corporations and even the Horned Cattle Fund, which in 1946 paid the entire prize list for livestock and provided an additional $150 grant, the tri-level government assistance allowed the directors to proceed with plans for expansion.

Those plans, understandably, focused on the agricultural components. The Manitoba Winter Fair continued its efforts to provide specific service to the agricultural community. The fair had provided a fall show and sale for livestock through most of the 1920s, 1930s and 1940s. In 1948, a similar event was staged, with an additional judging competition for Hampshire sheep and

ᏋᎯ *undated*

"A 26-year-old horse, competing against entries young enough to be its grand-children, proved that it's heart that counts as it captured the featured jumping event of the Thursday night light-horse show at the Manitoba Winter Fair, with a crowd of more than 5,000 in attendance, 'Bouncing Buster' of the Lilla-Gord Stables of Brandon, doyen of western Canadian jumping horses, captured the knock-down-and-out champion-ship after three extra jump-offs. And 5,000 hearts rode with the veteran performer over each jump."
from the *Brandon Sun*

a "Breeder Feeder Competition." Two years later, a separate December poultry show was staged. These additional speciality events demonstrated the winter fair's ongoing effort to promote the agricultural industry.

The winter fair itself was dominated by livestock and farm competitions, and the directors continued their efforts to expand and revise this aspect of their show. Consistent with the continuing emphasis on commercial livestock, the management added a special carcass class to the annual show in 1957. In this event, judging in the ring was matched with a second judging of the slaughtered carcass on the packer's rail. The innovations extended to the horse competitions as well. The assistance of the North Dakota Cutting Horse Association allowed the Manitoba Winter Fair to add a cutting horse demonstration to the 1955 show. It proved to be a crowd-pleasing event and returned to the fair for several more years.

The directors faced a special challenge in attempting to keep the poultry show buoyant. On an annual basis, director Bill Evans, known affectionately as "Mr. Chicken," kept the future of the poultry show on the association's agenda. There was good reason for debate. Forty years earlier, the poultry show attracted as many as 4,000 entries. By the mid-1950s, by which time commercial farms had taken over much of egg production and the average prairie farm could no longer boast of its own prize-winning flock of Rhode Island Reds or Wyandottes, a poultry show was of only marginal interest in the agricultural scheme of things. Commercial producers with giant flocks of battery hens were not likely to become regular exhibitors. Those persons who did exhibit were increasingly fanciers and hobbyists.

As interest in the poultry competitions waned, the directors wavered in the attention they paid to this competition, which many viewed as a pet show. Some years, they would offer classes during the winter fair for showbirds; other years they would underwrite a separate show, usually in early December. The directors had difficulty finding a permanent place for the poultry events, although they did take note of the interest among exhibitors.

THE MANITOBA WINTER FAIR'S COMMITMENT to agriculture faced the ultimate test in 1952. In the midst of planning for the winter show, word was received of an outbreak of hoof-and-mouth disease in Saskatchewan. The threat posed by the highly contagious disease made it impossible to hold cattle, sheep or swine events for that year. Faced with the loss of the livestock features, the directors decided to cancel the entire show, although they did run a fall show and a December poultry show.

With virtually no cash reserves to fall back upon, the winter fair association was forced to adopt desperate measures. It was impossible to cut costs by reducing staff, for they had no permanent employees of their own, only those they shared with the Provincial Exhibition. The president, Roy Clark attempted to get assurance from public agencies that their grants would continue, even in the absence of the show. What made the cancellation more galling was the loss of possible fresh support. D.G. Mackenzie, chairman of the Board of Grain Commissioners, had organized a special trainload of executives of Winnipeg agricultural companies to travel to Brandon for the fair. This excursion was cancelled when the fair was closed and was never attempted again.

There was concern over the next twelve months that the continuing threat from the disease would force cancellation of a second consecutive exhibition. Although they received assurances from government officials that the danger had passed, the directors remained uncertain. On the eve of the 1953 fair, new stories began to circulate that cattle entries were being sprayed with disinfectant. Some exhibitors became nervous with the fears of a recurrence of hoof-and-mouth disease. An announcement by federal veterinarians that such treatment was a normal precaution and that there was no reason for concern eventually placated the exhibitors and

124 *Agricultural commentator Lionel Moore interviews an exhibitor at the 1953 winter fair. Observers are Fred Dunn, on the left, and Les Hancock on the right.*

125   *The 4-H exhibit,
winter fair, 1953.*

126   *Manitoba Department
of Agriculture exhibit,
winter fair, 1953.*

ensured that the 1953 agricultural events went ahead as scheduled. The cancellation of the 1952 winter fair had been an unmitigated disaster, coming as it did at a time when the annual event was in financial straits. Assistance from the government and breed associations provided the cash necessary to carry on, and the winter fair was back on the track within a year. Faced with the same outbreak of hoof-and-mouth disease, the summer fair did not cease operations in 1952. Livestock competitions were cancelled, but the horse show was increased in size. That was also the year that the Manitoba Trade Show was first added to the program. Only committed cattle fanciers made much note of the absence of the livestock competitions, and the fair proceeded much as before, evidence of the lesser role assigned to agricultural events in the summer exhibition as opposed to their primary importance to the winter fair.

Livestock was not the only agricultural feature included in the winter fair. It was a matter of considerable local pride that the Seed Fair had been lured back to Brandon after several years in Winnipeg. The concerted effort of M.J. Tinline, superintendent of the Experimental Farm, succeeded in making this event a centre-piece of the 1947 exhibition and subsequent winter fairs.

The Manitoba Winter Fair was also constantly seeking ways to interest future farmers in their show. The 1948 winter fair included a "calf scurry," sponsored by the Aberdeen Angus Association, with the provision that winners had to show their calves the next year. As with the calf scramble hosted by the summer fair, this event found little support from the Manitoba Department of Agriculture, which considered it an entertainment event, and not an agricultural competition. However, in 1953, an offer by P.F. Ford, provincial agronomist, to sponsor a junior 4-H seed show gained wide approval, from both the fair directors and government officials. The feature attracted wide interest, with entries coming from the three prairie provinces and the Peace River district in northern British Columbia.

127 *A winter fair commit-
tee meeting in 1951. From
the left, M.J. Tinline, Charles
Good, Frank Anderson, Roy
Clark, Sid McLennan, Alice
Hogeland.*

160

Although agriculture continued to dominate the annual winter fair, the directors came to the sad realization during the 1950s that livestock and seeds were not enough to satisfy the urban audience and the fair relied on Brandon attendance to keep the event financially solvent. Attracting urban participation became, therefore, one of their prime objectives. There were efforts to secure additional attendance through advertising, although here the directors were caught in a classic bind. While attendance remained low, they did not have the funds for a proper publicity campaign; until they promoted their fair more aggressively, attendance was not likely to rise significantly. They did attempt to reach out to the United States, not through radio spots or full-page advertisements, but by inviting as guests for the bull sale all the county agricultural agents from Minnesota, Wisconsin and North and South Dakota.

The lack of an advertising budget was assisted by some notable corporate generosity. In the days leading up to the 1947 fair, and during the event itself, Brandon Packers dedicated its noon-hour broadcasts on radio station CKX to winter fair promotion. CKX was also carrying a feature in 1947 called "Who Am I," written by *Brandon Sun* journalist John A. MacNaughton, and sponsored by the board. As part of its community support for the fair, CKX offered the winter fair free advertising every morning after the major news casts, and also began in 1947 to provide live coverage of the official opening on Monday of fair week, and the crowning of the "Barley King" the next day. Under manager Alex McPhail, the promotional efforts branched out in new directions.

By the mid-1950s, the traditional newspaper ads were accompanied by radio "spots," brochures, window cards, even bumper stickers. A campaign with the March of Dimes in 1954, offering buyers chances to win one of three steers, five market lambs, five market hogs or a pony, raised more than $3,400 dollars for the fight against polio. The program was typical of the association's attempts to elevate its profile in the community, while in this instance simultaneously aiding a very worthwhile cause.

These efforts to increase attendance would only succeed if the audience were properly entertained and willing to return the following year. To accomplish this, it was essential that the winter fair program be broadened into more strictly "popular" events. The 1957 winter fair included a series of special events to celebrate the city's 75th anniversary. The fair opened with a parade which included every type of conveyance from the Red River cart and buckboard to the most modern vehicles. The evening show included just a hint of rodeo, with bucking broncos and Brahma bulls adding variety to the proceedings. Through the 1950s, special events from model airplane competitions to western dancing elimination contests were included in the program. The band of the 26th Field Regiment had, in the late 1940s, provided entertainment during the evening horse show. Some of the additions were less professional. Towards the end of the decade, the winter fair included a "mutt" show sponsored by Dr. Ballard's dog food company, hula hoop contests, and a dance competition featuring the latest craze, the twist. These attempts to popularize the winter fair were at least a modest success, but the directors continued the search for new elements and devices which would stimulate public, particularly urban, interest in their presentation.

Not all the directors welcomed these new departures, and particularly protested the addition of the obvious "crowd-pleasers" which strayed a long way from agriculture. After the 1956 fair, director James Moffatt complained that some items on the program were becoming altogether too trivial. While his fellow directors no doubt listened with respect to Moffatt's objections, they knew that attracting the urban audience was essential to the salvation of the winter fair and so such features were continued. Some of the attractions, however, and several of the commercial displays which filled the exhibit rooms in the winter fair buildings went too far. Following the 1956 show, the directors noted somewhat tersely that "it was the general opinion that novelties cheapened the exhibit."

Purity had its price, and the prospect of declining attendance and reduced revenues was something the directors were not prepared to tolerate. Although men such as Moffatt would continue their rear-guard effort to preserve the agricultural integrity of the show, market forces demanded an increasing effort to make the annual event more popular. It was necessary to branch out into fields of commercial enterprise and entertainment that earlier boards would not have accepted. Attendance and association profits climbed steadily through the first decade after World War II, although it would be wrong to attribute the increase to the addition of entertainment. As the directors would discover in the 1960s and 1970s, features like light horse competitions and Grand Prix jumping drew far more people than such temporary expedients as dance contests and musical performances.

As the winter fair grew, it found itself boxed in by its own facilities. What money the directors had for improvements to the facilities went to repair the aging buildings. Basically, the show had outgrown its home. Competitors had to be turned away each year as there was not enough space to accommodate them. The board at one time solved part of their problem by expanding across 11th Street into the Brandon Armoury. The building was used as a display space for carcasses and for meat-cutting demonstrations performed by J.C. Donaldson of Brandon Packers. Offering dressed meat as door prizes also ensured that the armoury events attracted a sizeable audience. After the 1958 fair, in another move forced by limited space, the directors reduced the number of entries allowed in a number of classes, including Belgian, Percheron and Clydesdale, until an $85,000 extension to the barns had been completed.

Such temporary arrangements did not solve the underlying

128 *R. Macpherson, winter fair president, 1953-56; Provincial Exhibition president, 1961-62.*

129 *Lil Williamson on Handy Andy, and Keith Macpherson on Stormy Weather at the summer fair.*

130 *"Two Little Girls in Blue," Randall and Shawn Carpenter, driving Mrs. Music, owned by Marshall Brook Farm, Winnipeg, at the 1959 winter fair.*

problem of lack of space. To make matters worse, the winter fair occasionally faced scheduling conflicts. The Wheat City Arena played host to the Brandon Wheat Kings and the fair dates frequently conflicted with the hockey schedule. On a fairly regular basis there would be a game—often an important play-off game—scheduled for the Saturday night before fair week. When this occurred, it left only a few hours in which to haul in the dirt which covered the ice surface in the main arena. The matter came to a head before the 1953 winter fair, when the directors requested access to the buildings for a week before and after the annual show, in accordance with the 1946 agreement which transferred control of the buildings to the City of Brandon. The protest appeared to have worked, for scheduling problems were resolved in time for the 1954 winter fair.

Although the Manitoba Winter Fair felt justified in requesting government assistance for either expansion of exisiting facilities—a difficult task given the property's downtown location—or construction of new fair buildings, their appeals fell on deaf ears. The winter fair would have to stay where it was, and somehow manage to squeeze an ever-expanding event into a small, tired facility.

By 1958, BRANDON'S TWO FAIRS found themselves on markedly different paths. The winter fair appeared to have come of age after decades as the proverbial "weak sister" of the two Brandon exhibitions. Attendance was increasing each year, and although the financial problems had not yet disappeared, a more solvent future seemed likely. The success of the winter fair seemed assured, and although purists grumbled about the addition of such "pop" events as dance and hula hoop contests, these events, combined with better advertising and more regular horse shows provided the directors with the audiences and the security necessary to plan for the future.

131 *Frank O. Meighen, barrister, solicitor, exhibition director and president. For years he was the attractions chairman when the grandstand shows were a major feature.*

132 *Wilfred McGregor, farmer, university governor, and for many years an exhibition director.*

133 *The directors of the Provincial Exhibition, 1956.*
Left to right, front row: Hope Turner, Maurice Evans, Wilmot McComb, Harvey Tolton, Frank Meighen (president), H.L. Crawford, Roy Clark.
Second row: Dave Brown, Dave Montgomery, Mac Brownridge, Bill Middleton, Bob McClement, Henry Rungay.
Third row: N.W. Kerr, Bob Smith, Bob Macpherson, Jim Moffatt, Alex McPhail, A.G. Cockerill, George MacArthur.
Fourth row: Avery Harrison, Bill McGregor, Roy Hopper, Archie Olson.

134 *Brandon delegates in Winnipeg, 1956, attending the convention of Western Canada Association of Exhibitions.*
Left to right:
Alex McPhail, H.L. Crawford, Carl Sedlmayr, Jr. of Royal American shows, F.O. Meighen, George MacArthur, Harvey Tolton.

135 *The entry of George McKenzie and Son, Brandon, in the 1959 winter fair.*

166

The success and stability of the winter show stood in marked contrast to the growing problems encountered at the Provincial Exhibition of Manitoba. By the mid-1950s, financial problems were already much in evidence. A summer storm in 1954 had reduced attendance for several days of the fair, resulting in a $10,000 loss on the year's proceedings. This loss forced the directors to make several deep cuts in the program for the following year, including the cancellation of the popular fireworks display. Attempts were made to counter the distressing trend toward lower attendance and reduced profits. The addition of more entertainment features and the expenditure of more money on advertising did not stem the tide.

As the dates for the 1958 fair approached, the directors were confident they had put their house back in order. Entries in the agricultural classes, typically a good barometer of public interest, were up significantly; space for outdoor concessions and church booths was fully subscribed and a number of excellent commercial exhibits had been secured. But the people stayed away. The drop was not cataclysmic, but revenue was down in all quarters. One year's decline did not constitute a trend, but coming on the heels of a general slackening in the exhibition's fortunes the returns offered some solemn portents for the future. The directors were not yet concerned with explaining the drop—although many fair-goers told them that they had finally tired of paying to see the "same old thing" year after year. Their short-term preoccupation was with improving the fortunes of the summer show and putting it back on the road to prosperity. However, that task would prove more difficult than they initially imagined, for a variety of forces, many beyond the control of the exhibition management, were conspiring to usurp the commercial and educational function of the annual summer event.

The 1950s had witnessed a major turning point. For decades the Manitoba Winter Fair had been an agricultural competition, of little more than passing interest to the people of Brandon, but one well-supported by the farmers and cattlemen of western Manitoba. Alterations in the winter fair program had brought the event more in step with popular tastes and had secured the fair greater attendance and more revenue. For the Provincial Exhibition, the trend was in the opposite direction. The formula which had worked so well for years was no longer effective. The decline was not precipitous, for the summer fair continued to hold an honoured place with the people of Brandon and surrounding districts. But interest in the event was definitely waning, and the continued efforts of fair management to resurrect the event consistently fell short. These changes had only begun in the 1950s. The process would continue over the next twenty years.

136   *Closing ceremonies at the winter fair.*

137   *A hackney class at the evening horse show, winter fair, c.1951.*

168

Chapter Five

1961·1985

Years of Transition

THE END OF THE 1950s saw the Provincial Exhibition of Manitoba at its peak. Attendance improved year by year; applause was heard from all quarters for the quality of the entertainment and the continued commitment to agriculture. It was a heady time to be associated with the fair, for the future indeed looked bright. Even the winter fair, though a more modest undertaking, had earned its share of kudos through the 1950s and seemed headed for even brighter days.

Those involved with Brandon's fair would have been hard pressed to predict the turbulent times which lay ahead. The successes of the past would not be readily reproduced, and the years ahead proved more difficult than expected. The summer fair, long the crowning glory of Brandon's year, struggled through hard times before it once again found its feet. The winter fair, long the quiet partner, would steadily progress towards a larger share of the limelight.

The change was hard to identify and emerged only slowly. Visitors to the 1961 summer fair, for example, probably saw few of the underlying problems surrounding the Provincial Exhibition. That fair had much more in common with the glory days of the mid-1950s than the troubled shows to follow. George Hees, Canada's minister of trade and commerce. presided over the festivities. The highlight of the show was the Western Canada Trade Show. The brand new $30,000 building built specially for this show was crammed with exhibits from western Canadian manufacturers.

Most patrons headed directly for the midway, forsaking the commercial and agricultural exhibits until their appetite for Royal American's rides, games and peep shows had been satisfied. The "girlie" shows, as always, attracted more than a respectable share of attention. Many clucked in disapproval at the licentious excesses promised by the shills for Club Lido or the all-black Harlem in Havana, but the long line-ups of slightly embarrassed men suggested the shows had found their natural audience.

138　*A Travellers' Day Parade on modern Rosser Avenue. This six-horse hitch belongs to Aubrey Toll, Blyth, Ontario, in the driver's seat. Mr. and Mrs. Ed. McManus, of Labatt's, are the passengers.*

139　*4-H club activities were a major feature of summer fairs during the 1960s and 1970s.*

140 *At some fairs, as many as 2000 4-H club members were present for province-wide rallies.*

Before the lifting of the curtain on the grandstand show, most fair-goers found time to wander through the livestock exhibits, commercial displays, government presentations and other attractions. Although they lacked the popular appeal of the midway, the agricultural attractions maintained a devoted following. The 4-H events, with a record 2500 competitors, showcased lively and promising battles between Manitoba's future farmers. On the race track, events like the Manitoba Colt Futurity drew thousands of racing fans.

As had become standard fare, each days' festivities were capped with an evening grandstand performance. In 1961, Homer and Jethro and the elegantly attired June Taylor Dancers were the centerpieces of "Away We Go," a gala presentation played on the outdoor stage erected in front of the grandstand. Those who had put in a full day at the summer exhibition left the grounds exhausted from the excitement, novelty and thrills, but anxious to return for those things missed on the first go-round.

The artistic and financial success of the 1961 summer fair obscured its serious structural weaknesses. Over the next decade and a half, the directors would have to accept that the halcyon days of the grandstand performance had passed; find a replacement for the extremely popular Royal American Shows; struggle with impending bankruptcy; repair or replace the aging buildings, all while maintaining the support and appeal which the fair had enjoyed for over 60 years.

The superficial buoyancy of the 1961 fair hid some distressing portents. The number of beef and dairy cattle entries had dipped alarmingly. The harness racing events organized by the "Speed" Committee recorded a loss of $2,300. Income from the concession stands dipped some $2,000 from the previous year, and the loud protests from commercial exhibitors over increasing display costs raised concerns that exhibit space would prove more difficult to sell in subsequent years. The exhibition was in some trouble. At the annual meeting, finance chairman J. Lawson Valens summarized the year's returns: final totals indicated a net loss of $6,500. That sum itself was hardly devastating, but combined with other signs of decline, the message was not a happy one.

The problems facing the Provincial Exhibition of Manitoba did not suddenly appear in 1961. Signs of impending crisis had first emerged in the late 1950s, at the height of the show's popularity. The decline of the summer fair had more to do with changing times than decisions taken by the fair directors. In 1955, CKX Television opened in Brandon. The entertainment-based summer fair faced an unprecedented challenge. The annual grandstand show, once the highlight of the entertainment scene in the area, now went head to head with Jackie Gleason, Gunsmoke, I Love Lucy, the Plouffe Family, and the Ed Sullivan Show. The summer fair, and to a lesser extent the winter show, were no longer the only shows in town!

Other implications emerged rather more slowly. In the past, promoters of new inventions, from farm machinery to the vacuum cleaner and, ironically, the television set, had depended on displays at the exhibitions to tout their wares. Dozens of companies had rented exhibit space to take advantage of the unique opportunity to reach thousands of fair-goers. Suddenly, television provided a better and cheaper alternative; potential customers could be reached in their homes daily, rather than once during a hectic week at the fair.

AS THE YEARS PASSED, 'progress' conspired against the summer extravaganza. Improvements to Manitoba's highway system, better cars and cheap gas brought the cultural, commercial and entertainment events in Winnipeg and other centers within comparatively easy reach. Further expansion of television service, the addition of new radio stations and a proliferation of commercial entertainments in Brandon and surrounding towns all lessened the dependence on the summer fair.

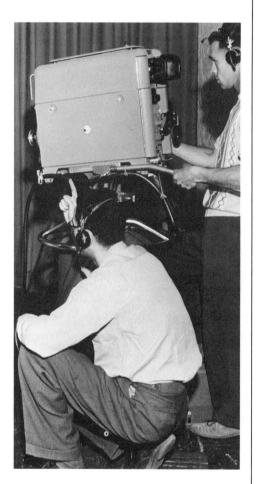

141 *Television was both a friend and a foe in the 1950's. 'Grandstand'-type shows on TV drained the summer fairs' audiences, while informative programming was both enlightening and entertaining. Here, Lionel Moore gets the latest fair report from livestock commissioner John Connor and Fair manager Alex McPhail, c.1954.*

175

Signs that the exhibition was facing a fall from grace emerged as early as 1958. A survey of the grounds in the summer of that year revealed the need for extensive renovation of almost all buildings. The exhibition had been receiving an annual grant of $8,600 from the City of Brandon, an amount matched dollar for dollar by the federal government. With a view to completing these improvements, the board applied for a continuation of that arrangement. As the Brandon *Sun* reported :

> Much pressed for revenue, the exhibition needs the financial support of the citizens of Brandon....Without this financial support, the exhibition would find it difficult to continue.

The newspaper's editor lent the weight of his editorial column to the cause, reminding his readers that:

> The exhibition is a Brandon institution by birth, upbringing and maturity, and represents an important factor in the continued growth of the community.

The exhibition association left little to chance. A full page advertisement in the newspaper reminded citizens of the upcoming bylaw vote. A banner headline, playing on age-old rivalries, asked for public support: "THE PROVINCIAL EXHIBITION OF MANITOBA IS AN INSTITUTION WHICH THE CITIZENS OF BRANDON MUST JEALOUSLY GUARD LEST IT BE LOST TO WINNIPEG". An open letter which reminded voters that the by-law asked only for the continuation of an existing arrangement which would bring a matching sum to the community in the form of federal grants. It also noted:

> The Provincial Exhibition of Manitoba is recognized as the outstanding agricultural show in Western Canada. It is one of Brandon's largest industries and the grounds constitute the city's finest park.

Confident they had done all that was necessary to secure the passage of the bylaw, the directors waited for the results to be counted.

The newspaper referred to voting day, 29 October 1958, as

Black Tuesday. Only 20% of the eligible voters turned out, and those who marked their ballots rejected three out of five money bylaws. Grants for Brandon College and Fairview Home received the required majority vote. The other proposals, the Provincial Exhibition grant, money for storm sewers and an east-end swimming pool, failed to get the 60% necessary for their passage. The exhibition bylaw found its greatest support among residents of the south and west ends of the city. Voters in the north and the east turned thumbs down on their request by a sizable margin. On a city-wide basis, the bylaws for the fair and the pool did not even secure majority approval. It was a devastating blow, and the fact that only one fifth of the eligible voters had even bothered to register their opinions hardly eased the pain.

The editor of the *Brandon Sun* was caustic in his response to the failure of the storm sewer and exhibition bylaws. Reflecting on the city's history of building for the future, he said:

> People talked less of "progress" then, but their thinking and their actions were more "modern" than ours. The fact is that with all our present-day material comforts and opulence we are growing soft, lazy, selfish. Our thinking tends to centre more and more around our egotistic requirements and to heck with everything else. This is a dangerous, short-sighted, irresponsible attitude. Let us hope that the election debacle will help to wake us up while there may still be time to save Brandon from slumping into a backwater place to be avoided by all who are able to see Canada's future beyond their own backyards.

Exhibition directors doubtlessly shared these harsh sentiments. They still needed the money, but were reluctant to once again approach the city for support. Brief consideration was given to discontinuing operations, more a reflection of their melancholy state than a realistic option. It was decided instead to negotiate a $50,000 mortgage, offering the exhibition property as collateral. By raising the money in this manner, the directors added to the yearly financial burden, but were able to secure the federal government's matching grant. Thus, despite the stringing rebuke it had suffered, the Provincial Exhibition put together the money it needed for improvements.

The bylaw defeat made the exhibition directors wary. Wilfred McGregor, a farmer and long-time board member, reminded board members several times over the next few years of the obvious "apathy" in the city towards the summer fair, and suggested that they direct their attentions to educating the public on the exhibition's contributions.

ANOTHER SENIOR BOARD MEMBER, Brandon lawyer Frank O. Meighen, warned of a different crisis due to strike at any moment. Speaking from his position as attractions chairman, Mr. Meighen called on board members to begin considering future directions. Though he noted that all agreed that the yearly grandstand shows were first rate productions, the balance sheet screamed for change. The costs for decent grandstand acts were rising steadily, revenues from admission fees and concession charges were declining, and there was no likelihood that fair patrons would pay more for the attractions.

Meighen easily substantiated his warning. The grandstand attractions for 1961 had cost more than $15,000, an increase of over $500 from the previous year. Additional staff requirements and extras such as the fireworks display had added to the financial burden. The outlook for the future was foreboding. In December 1961, Frank Meighen attended the annual meeting of the Western Canada Association of Exhibitions and based on his discussions with representatives from other western fairs, reported back that the cost for grandstand attractions for 1962 was expected to top $20,000.

For many years, the attractions chairmen from the Class "A" circuit in Western Canada, men like Brandon's Meighen, had worked together in contracting the grandstand attractions. By

1962 29 January
  The board of the winter fair has issued a gate pass and reserved seat to Mr. George Stewart of Pilot Mound, who has attended every winter fair since its inception.

1964 14 March
  The board of the winter fair is advised that Barclay Creighton has not missed a fair since its inception.

142 *A typical grandstand presentation in the mid-1950s.*

143 *A poster depicting a grandstand act from the late 1960s.*

144 *When Gene Holter had his wild animal act at the 1968 exhibition, he offered members of the board an opportunity to ride the elephant. It was generally agreed by the passengers that in the future they'd stick to horses.*

buying together, the fairs in Brandon, Regina, Saskatoon, Calgary and Edmonton could provide prairie audiences with some of the best entertainment on the continent. The process was simple, and had undergone few variations since its inception prior to the First World War. Each December, the attractions chairmen attended the annual meeting of the Showmens' League of America, a Chicago-based entertainment association. During their stay, the representatives watched the latest variety acts and listened to the impresarios as they competed for the five-week grandstand contract. The committee members from the western Canadian circuit then assembled what they viewed as the most popular package of musical acts, performing animals, and acrobatic troupes, with a high-wire dare-devil act usually thrown in for a heart-stopping finale.

The evening grandstand show had drawn a large and dedicated audience for over fifty years. Its mystique lay in part in the fact it was held on an open-air stage, prey to the vagaries of prairie weather. Seated in the grandstand, patrons looked north over the racetrack, their eyes scanning across the racing stables to fix on the Brandon skyline, dominated by the large brick edifice of Mackenzie Seeds. In front of them, on the infield side of the race track stood the stage, flanked at the sides and rear by a garish and well-lit set. A battery of lights and artwork, carefully designed to match the year's theme, set the stage.

On many occasions, powerful winds threatened to bring down the backdrop, while at other times a sudden downpour would send jugglers, dancers and musicians running for cover beneath the grandstand building. Patrons whose tickets could not be honored because of a rain-out were told to come back the next night, when a double-header was staged to "make-good." There was little grumbling from an audience well-used to living with the capricious prairie environment.

But other days, when the massive prairie sky held the deep blue of a summer night, the evening grandstand show would bring

145 *Henry Rungay, president, Provincial Exhibition, 1962-64.*

179

to the fair patrons a world of sensational delights. As the distant horizon advanced upon the setting sun, the lighted stage would begin to glow, and then to radiate, as the extravaganza engulfed the willing audience with a flood of escapism, frivolity, treacherous thrills and pure enjoyment.

Sunday evenings had their own special events. Thousands crammed into the grandstand the Sunday before the fair started for an ecumenical church service, dominated by choral performances and hymn singing. The grandstand provided a majestic setting for this outpouring of spiritual brotherhood. It was a fitting part of the week's festivities, a somewhat serious yet joyous celebration of the gifts to be witnessed during the fair.

The glory days had come and gone, and in the early 1970s, the exhibition directors were compelled to pull down the final curtain on an important Western Manitoba institution. Soaring costs, declining interest, and the implacable competition from television and radio had slowly eroded the returns from the event. The death warrant, though, was signed by the provincial government when, in 1974, the department of labor condemned the aging grandstand. Without the money to effect the necessary repairs, and finally convinced that Frank Meighen's warnings of 1961 had come true, the directors decided not to repair or rebuild the grandstand and so ended the long summer of western Manitoba's favorite show.

It had to end, but many would mourn its passing. For years, the arc lights, costumes, performers and music had coalesced to transport the collective imagination of the patrons into that make-believe world of show business. When all these elements combined, and their impact seemed even more powerful against the magnificent backdrop of the prairie night-fall, the grandstand show projected a tremendous power, capable for a few hours at least of helping the audience forget such mundane things as rust, drought, grasshoppers and even mortgages. There were many happy

146 *D.C. Lawson, president, Provincial Exhibition, 1967-69, won high acclaim for his chairmanship of the Keystone building committee.*

147 *K.T. Macpherson, light-horse exhibitor, director, president Provincial Exhibition 1969-70, 1971-72.*

memories resonating through the decaying seats and bent girders of the old grandstand, and only a few "progressives" were genuinely happy to see the building torn down. To many, the loss of the grandstand signaled the end of the fair as they knew it.

The exhibition directors knew the risk they were taking in tearing down the grandstand, and also knew the necessity of charting a different course for the future of the fair. A substitute had to be found for the night show, so the Brandon fair joined the western Canada rodeo circuit. Broncos and steer wrestlers replaced jugglers and dancing bears.

THE LOSS OF THE GRANDSTAND SHOW was but one sign of the changing times, for the late 1960s and early 1970s would see many alterations in the traditional pattern. For many years, the Royal American Shows' carnival had formed the centerpiece for the annual festivities. In 1966, that participation came to an end. The passing was noted with sadness. On 26 November 1971, Director Hope Turner commented that:

> We've never had a fair since we lost Royal American.

In giving silent support to this utterance, other board members were prepared to forgive the hyperbole.

Certainly there had been fairs since Royal American deserted Brandon in favour of the larger audiences of Winnipeg's Red River Exhibition, a double blow in that Brandon hated to lose anything to the provincial capital. But they had not been the same. Hope Turner, a Carroll district farmer and long-time horse exhibitor, had merely echoed a popular public sentiment.

The association between the Tampa-based Royal American, led by its flamboyant owner Carl J. Sedlmayr, and the Provincial Exhibition had seemed etched in stone. It had been a profitable arrangement for both; the Brandon exhibition provided large and enthusiastic audiences while Royal American's participation put

148 *Rodeo action at the "ex".*

149 *Scenes from the 1972 exhibition midway.*

the western Manitoba show on the map. Sedlmayr was a widely acclaimed promoter, called the 'King of the Carnivals' by *Billboard Magazine*. The title was well-deserved, for his well-honed promotion skills drew thousands to fair-grounds across Canada and the United States. He knew how to pack them in. Royal American represented a blend of the exotic and the quixotic, with ample portions of thrills and games of chance thrown in for good effect. Fair audiences were also titillated by the risque, coy and charming performance of such famous ladies of the strip-tease as Sally Rand and Gypsy Rose Lee.

Without a great deal of warning, Sedlmayr informed the directors he would not be back the following year. The Winnipeg fair, a frequent rival of the Brandon fair, though no match in its agricultural events, had stolen the crown jewel of the western Manitoba show. It was a cruel blow to an exhibition already reeling from the declining interest in the grandstand show. The single most important attraction on the grounds, and a crowd favorite for years, had left Brandon for Winnipeg.

The exhibition directors scrambled for a suitable replacement. There were only a few carnival shows available, and over the next two decades, the Brandon fair tried several of them. They were not, however, Royal American, as patrons reminded fair management every year. In rapid succession, the carnivals led by William T. Collins, Bernard Thomas, Sonny Meyers, and Ray Cammack were tried and, for one reason or another, found wanting. Although the summer fair was clearly on the decline, the directors still felt a suitable carnival attraction could resurrect the exhibition's flagging fortunes.

Many continued to pine for the return of Royal American, believing that only the time-honored favorite could take the Brandon fair back to the glory days. In 1974, they changed their tune, for Royal American was in serious trouble.

It was a spectacular fall from grace. At 2 a.m., on the morning of 24 July 1975, a combined force of Edmonton City Police and Royal Canadian Mounted Police raided the Edmonton midway offices and seized Royal American's business files. In short order, Canadian taxation officials laid a number of charges of fraud against Royal American and several individuals associated with the independent carnival exhibitors who followed the Royal American circuit.

The court trials, lost in a quagmire of charges and counter-charges, dragged on without an official resolution. To rescue the case from the mess, the Alberta government appointed Supreme Court Justice Laycraft as a one-man royal commission on Royal American. In his summation a year later, Justice Laycraft concluded that Royal American had been a "malignant force" in the communities in which it had operated. He cited numerous cases of calculated bribery, involving cash as well as expensive gifts, through which Sedlmayr and his executives curried favor with exhibition boards and local politicians. Though the charges were stayed, Royal American withdrew from the Canadian exhibition circuit.

While the demise of Royal American may have left the Brandon exhibition relieved in that the show was no longer associated with their fair, the dilemma of the continuing decline of the Brandon summer show remained. They eventually found an answer. Canada's Conklin Brothers' Shows, who proclaim themselves the largest exhibition company in North America, had provided the midway on the Class "A" circuit during World War I. Conklin now added the Brandon fair to their summer schedule. Since Conklin already held contracts for such prestigious fairs as the Canadian National Exhibition and the Pacific National Exhibition, addition of their carnival indicated that Brandon had found its way back onto the major midway circuit.

The battle to regain lost status and, even more importantly, lost patrons, proved to be a difficult one. The problem lay in finding a new purpose and direction. The mix of entertainment, commercial displays and agricultural competitions had worked well in the past, but the formerly potent combination now seemed stale,

150　*More than 50 tons of horses were on parade in front of the grandstand one evening during the 1967 show.*

🐌 *1978 21 June*

A column by Garth Stouffer noted: "The end of anything means a time for soul-searching in a quest for answers to why things were not better than they were... why didn't people show up? What were they looking for? What did we do wrong?

On the grounds and in the offices of the Provincial Exhibition of Manitoba, where a lot of people are no doubt wondering what they have to do to get crowds out, perhaps they'll listen to a few suggestions that have come to me in the days of the annual summer fair.

A number of people, it seems, remember the days when various church groups were the people who fed the multitudes...and a lot of well-pleased palates of yesteryear have fond recollections

151   *One of the competitors in the horseshoe-pitching contest, Provincial Exhibition.*

desperately in need of revitalization. The exhibition directors fought back, trying new attractions, expanding the list of special events, trying to recapture the special place the fair had long held in the hearts and minds of fairgoers.

WHILE THE SUMMER FAIR SANK into the doldrums, the winter fair was gradually emerging as the star of the two Brandon exhibitions. The decline of the summer extravaganza had a lot to do with increasing competition for the entertainment dollar. The gathering success of the winter show, ironically, reflected the fact that the directors had largely avoided entertainment and had adhered strictly to their agricultural message.

There was a clear message in this rather odd development, one that other exhibitions would have been wise to observe. The Brandon summer fair was not the only show to fall on hard times. Most of the major exhibitions, including the Edmonton, Calgary and Vancouver shows, faced crises of varying proportions during the 1960s and 1970s. Like Brandon, their facilities needed to be replaced, attendance either dropped or did not keep pace with financial needs, and they faced increasing criticism of their entertainment-based exhibitions. 'The agricultural fair is dead,' wrote critics across the west; their analysis was a little faulty.

Agricultural exhibitors were — and are — consistently among the most loyal fair supporters. The long list of Brandon exhibitors, both for the winter and summer fair, who have competed at the fair for forty years or more provides ample evidence of that support. As well, the agricultural events attracted thousands of dollars in grants and prizes from agricultural associations, companies and governments. The fact that a fair hosted a major agricultural competition provided ample justification for governments to underwrite the costs of new buildings and facilities. Perhaps of even greater importance, farm families have been the most loyal patrons of the exhibition, coming for the agricultural competitions, but staying to enjoy the entire extravaganza.

THE SIGNIFICANCE OF THIS FARM SUPPORT was not lost on the promoters of the Manitoba Winter Fair. While attendance at the summer show stagnated, the loyal exhibitors and patrons of the winter fair ensured that it enjoyed steady, if unspectacular growth. It continued to grow because it was a farmers' show, fulfilling their needs by providing an appropriate blend of competition, education, commercial display and entertainment, with the last being only a minor part of the whole.

In a series of speeches, managing director P. Alex McPhail had little difficulty defending the integrity of the winter event. The purpose of the fair, to his mind, was two-fold: to encourage improvement in agriculture and to better rural and urban life. The winter show was not an off-season variation of the summer exhibition. By McPhail's definition, the Provincial Exhibition was a "production" show, highlighting breeding stock. The winter fair had a different goal, where producers of cattle, poultry, pigs and seed displayed the finished products from their feeding and breeding programs. McPhail also acknowledged that such events as the light-horse shows, while not strictly agricultural, had an important role to play in that they attracted crowds. The admission revenues provided the money for the less glamorous but more important parts of the show. Like many other winter fair traditionalists, McPhail drew the line at the addition of contests, games and other attractions of a clearly entertainment nature. The traditionalists would have to bend a little as the time passed.

FOR THE TIME BEING, a more pressing problem, lack of space, continued to haunt the winter fair. The show was growing in importance and popularity, but did not have the ability to expand its quarters. The Wheat City Arena, bounded by 10th and 11th streets and Victoria and McTavish avenues, and surrounded by

of those good food days. As a matter of fact, a number of folks have mentioned the 'good old days' of the church booths during the past week... their mouths fairly drooling with the memories.

Nor could even the reminder that the various ethnic booths were doing a fair business...both on the midway and downstairs in the Festival 1978 area of the hitching ring...could wipe out memories of the days when the best cooks of every congregation would fairly outdo themselves in providing mouthwatering goodies in the cramped, hot and perhaps less than ideal quarters located in the buildings that once ringed the little show ring east of the mall grandstand."
from the *Brandon Sun.*

ૐ *1985 23 March*

In an interview with a Brandon journalist, Jack Simpson, retired manager of the Keystone Centre, recalled an unusual event from the old Wheat City Arena. A young "harum-scarum" went aloft in the steel girders which arched from one side of the arena to the other. To the great delight of the crowd, the venturesome one not only refused to come down, but managed to elude all efforts by the city's finest to capture him.

152 *Two aerial views: grounds and racetrack, c.1965, and Wheat City arena and winter fair buildings, taken some time after the roller rink was added in 1960.*

an expanding commercial and residential area, presented few options for expansion.

The increased demands for exhibit space placed the association directors in an awkward position. While they were pleased that their large and loyal following had convinced numerous commercial firms to apply for display locations, they were nonetheless concerned that they could not accommodate the steadily increasing demands. By 1964, the matter had become critical. Several board members raised the possibility of excluding commercial displays which did not relate to agriculture. A lengthy and convoluted discussion soon demonstrated how impossible it was to arrive at suitable criterion. While some argued that displays of electrical appliances could be curtailed, others quickly rebuffed the suggestion. While some felt such exhibits were urban in focus, many exhibitors tailored their presentations to rural patrons who were not exposed as regularly to corporate advertising.

The debate had only indicated the need for a suitable resolution to the problem. After considering the problem for a few years, the directors came up with an interim solution. By 1968, they had constructed a walkway across 11th street, connecting the Wheat City Arena with the Armory, which was then turned into a display room. While this temporary expansion of the fairgrounds worked moderately well for the fair, area residents were of another mind. The walkway blocked local access, and several families were forced to make lengthy detours to their homes. The fair attempted to mollify the people with admission passes and reserve tickets for the horse show. Ewart Abey, a winter fair director, offered a more personal touch, visiting each household to explain the necessity of closing the street in the interest of serving agriculture.

Such stop-gap measures did not resolve the underlying problems. Everyone involved with the fair agreed something had to be done about the building. The aging structure needed major renovations and more space was required, though it was doubtful

that the current grounds would accommodate any new buildings. The solution came up unexpectedly, forcing fast decisions and major changes on both the winter and the summer exhibitions.

Early in the 1960s, a number of winter fair directors, especially Alex McPhail and Reginald Forbes, voiced their concerns about the Wheat City Arena. Without an early re-location of the fair, they argued, the entire enterprise could well be doomed. Though the fair continued to be a success, the cramped quarters and hefty repair bills kept the winter fair running continually in the red. It was a tired old structure, situated on a valuable piece of downtown property, and it did not allow for the expansion of the fair grounds. The call was out for a new facility.

The first concerted move toward a new exhibition building was made on 12 November 1963. Winter fair President George MacArthur, backed by two vice-presidents, Hope Turner and Reginald Forbes and managing director Alex McPhail, hosted a dinner meeting at the Prince Edward Hotel. Their invited guests included representatives of the City of Brandon, service clubs, the Chamber of Commerce, the media, and all the major cultural and agricultural groups who could conceivably be interested in using expanded exhibition buildings. MacArthur announced that the time to act had arrived. The news from Winnipeg was ominous. A group of promoters had plans to sponsor what they called the "Western Royal," a major horse show which threatened to challenge the Brandon show.

McPhail made the first move for the board. He commissioned the Winnipeg research firm of Hedlin, Menzies and Associates to study the need for a new home for agricultural displays. Their report was issued in 1966 and supported the winter fair board's claims that a new facility was amply justified. Nothing came of it immediately, in part because Mayor Magnacca believed that the WestMan Centennial Auditorium had a higher priority than a new fair building. Initial plans called for a proper auditorium to be included in the central exhibition structure, but Magnacca

153 *James I. Moffatt,*
exhibitor, director, winter fair
president, 1957-60, 1970-71.

favored a separate structure on the Brandon College grounds.

The impetus for more rapid action came from an unlikely source. Inspectors with the Manitoba department of labour had discovered serious structural faults in the steel and brickwork on the west side of the Wheat City Arena. Unless repairs were made soon, the building would have to be closed. A quick investigation revealed that the cost of the needed repairs would be prohibitive. The winter fair board responded by striking a special committee, with *Brandon Sun* vice-president F. McGuinness as chairman, to investigate prospects for building a replacement. Director Douglas Lawson was chosen for the onerous task of leading the vital building committee. Opinions were solicited from potential users on the size, location and nature of the proposed structure.

While the various committees continued their informal investigations, the board again commissioned Hedlin, Menzies and Associates of Winnipeg to appraise the community's needs. The Hedlin, Menzies report confirmed what many directors had concluded privately. A single building, properly designed and located, could serve the needs of both the summer and the winter fair. They also reported that paying for such a facility would not be easy in a community Brandon's size. Because of the anticipated problems of securing enough events to pay for the costs of construction, the consultants noted that it was imperative the building be debt-free the day it opened.

This rather cautious conclusion was borne out by a second professional study commissioned by the Keystone Committee. A well-known fund-raising firm, Brakeley and Co. of Montreal, had been hired to investigate potential sources of money for the facility. In their initial appraisal, submitted in June 1970, they foresaw donations of $1,250,000, one-fifth from firms and individuals in the Brandon area, $500,000 from national firms, with the remainder to come from the three levels of government. Firmly but gently, the Brakeley report also confirmed the cautionary note submitted by Hedlin, Menzies; the finished complex would not be able to

154 *George MacArthur, heavy-horse exhibitor, director, general manager, and president, winter fair, 1961-64.*

155 *R.H. Turner, heavy horse exhibitor, director of the winter fair and president, 1964-67.*

156 *R.E. Forbes, agrologist, extension specialist, president of the winter fair, 1967-69. He pledged himself to the amalgamation of the summer and winter fairs and was instrumental in helping this happen.*

157 *Advertisement in the 1965 winter fair program, promoting construction of a Keystone Center.*

service any long-term debt, making it imperative that initial fund-raising cover the entire cost of construction.

Planning for the Keystone Centre continued at two different levels; Douglas Lawson and his building committee spearheaded the design and construction end, while a separate finance committee worked out the monetary details.

Lawson, a second-generation Brandon implement dealer, drew on the ideas of literally thousands of individuals as he and his associates designed a multi-purpose community facility. During this formative phase, rough plans and finished blueprints were shown to and discussed with virtually every organization and interest group involved in an effort to ensure that the final product would be as functional as possible.

The fund-raising drive was equally inspired and wide-ranging. The vice-president of Western Manitoba Broadcasters, Stuart Craig, was recruited in October of 1970, and within weeks he in turn had selected chairmen and members for 15 separate committees. Their work was given a welcome boost when the Honorable W. J. McKeag, lieutenant-governor of Manitoba, accepted the honorary chairmanship, and J. Elmer Woods, a respected Winnipeg business leader, became honorary treasurer. The Brakeley Company established a Brandon office to assist with local solicitations and fund-raising events.

A project of this magnitude could not proceed without some opposition and controversy, and the Keystone Centre proved no exception. Brandon's mayor, W.K. Wilton, became concerned that the fund-raising program would fall short of its objective, potentially leaving the city with the task of finishing and then subsidizing the expensive and risky undertaking. Wilton used his considerable influence to bring the project to a temporary halt in the summer of 1971, and when work resumed the initial plans had been scaled down somewhat and several features, including a swimming pool and dining room, had been dropped. Even with these deletions, the final estimates still called for a $4.5 million building.

Although the fund raising proved extremely difficult, committee members were delighted with the local response. The money came in bundles large and small, as organizations around the area stepped forward to support the community project. The site of the condemned Wheat City Arena was sold to Canada Safeway, and the proceeds of $250,000 were turned over to the building fund by the City of Brandon. The winter fair, soon to be the major beneficiary of the new building, donated $50,000 from its reserves. The Brandon Kinsmen continued a long association with both the exhibition and community facilities by offering a grant of $75,000.

In total, some $900,000 came forward in this fashion, as groups large and small, well-endowed and impoverished, came forward to help. The Brandon Light Horse Society cleaned out its bank account and donated $1,000 to the project. The fund-raising efforts snowballed. School children sold their comic books and delivered the proceeds to the Keystone office. "White elephant" auctions were held in communities across southern Manitoba, including one memorable sale during which the public sale of donated beer was declared illegal by liquor inspectors. A group of students at Brandon University took pledges on how long they could live in an igloo built on the campus lawn. Senior citizens dipped into their pension income; 4-H members shared what they could out of their weekly allowances.

The beleagured workers on the various Keystone committees took heart from this welcome and overwhelming outpouring of support and encouragement. They knew their bank account was short of money to cover the costs of completing the centre, but they also knew the public solidly backed their continued efforts. Still, sympathy did not pay for girders and plywood and the Keystone Committees turned with anticipation to the government.

THE VOCAL ENTHUSIASM OF AREA RESIDENTS was not matched by federal and provincial politicians. Despite repeated and direct requests to the federal government, financial aid was not immediately forthcoming. Similarly, attempts to interest Manitoba Premier Walter Weir in the project faltered during the first year of the fund-raising campaign. However, Stuart Craig's spirited band of enthusiasts would keep trying.

The much needed break came, appropriately, during fair week in 1969. The president of the recently combined board of the summer and winter fairs, James I. Moffat, learned that the new Manitoba cabinet of Premier Ed Schreyer was enjoying a pre-session retreat in a residence at Brandon University. Always one to take the initiative, Moffat sent a courier to the politicians, inviting them to a cocktail party in the late afternoon and requesting that they allow themselves to be presented to the crowd at the evening grandstand performance.

The informality of the cocktail circuit hid any formal record of what transpired during the fair-time gathering. Local folklore suggests that the exhibition directors cornered the cabinet ministers and requested confirmation that the $1 million grant previously offered by Conservative premier Walter Weir would be honored. New to their jobs, and anxious to reassure Manitobans that business would proceed much as before even with the change of government, Schreyer and his colleagues agreed to the commitment. That such a guarantee had never been given was confirmed later when the new premier and his associates failed to find mention of the pledge in the official government records.

Fred Cleverley, editorial writer for the *Winnipeg Free Press,* delighted in informing his readership of Brandon's fast movers:

> There are people in Brandon who even use the word "hornswoggle" in a positive way, when they talk about how the Keystone Crew managed to turn something that was only a vague political suggestion from former premier Walter Weir into a multi-million dollar commitment from Ed Schreyer.

The political nuances and controversies soon faded. The flurry of activity at the summer fair grounds, and the slowly emerging structure demonstrated to Western Manitobans that they were about to get what they had paid and worked for. With justifiable pride, and loud collective sigh of relief, the Keystone Committee watched Brandon's largest community facility take shape. Both the summer and winter fairs had found a new home, and both would change rapidly to take advantage of the new opportunities presented by the Keystone Centre.

All this lay in the future. The Keystone Centre was open for business by the fall on 1972. The first hockey game was played in the new facility on 14 October, with Winnipeg Jet star Bobby Hull handling the ceremonial face-off in the Western Hockey League game. The official opening was held in conjunction with the commencement of the 1973 winter fair. Dignitaries including Governor General Roland Michener and Mrs. Michener, Hon. Eugene Whelan, Hon. James Richardson, Hon. Len Evans and a host of local politicians and community leaders gathered for a night of pageantry and celebration. The official ribbon-cutting ceremony was performed with a unique but appropriate twist. A large ribbon was stretched across the arena. A six-horse team, driven by Roland Michener with the help of long-time exhibitor and fair director Gordon Church, drove through the ribbon, thus declaring the facility and the 1973 fair open. The celebrations fit the new facility. The Keystone was a monument, but not to the politicians. It reflected the energy and commitment of the long-serving workers on the numerous Keystone committees and the enthusiatic support of Brandon and area residents. The night belonged to them.

The new Keystone Centre, complete with meeting rooms, arena, and a series of exhibition halls, offered exciting prospects for Brandon's fairs. Several aging buildings on the Summer Fair grounds could now be phased out or, even better, torn down. The multi-purpose Keystone could be readily adapted for the use of both exhibitions, and the greatly expanded space offered ample room for improvements and growth.

158　*An architect's depiction of the Keystone Centre.*

159　*During the period in which the Keystone was under construction, the winter fairs were held in the Man-Ex Arena in Exhibition Park. This small facility, with seating for only 1500, also served during this time as Brandon's main hockey arena.*

160   *Hon. Sam Uskiw, Manitoba Minister of Agriculture, uses an early form of motive power to turn the sod for the ultra-modern Keystone Centre, 12 November, 1970.*

161   *Surveying the Keystone under construction: R.E. Forbes, His Honor, Lieut-Governor W.J. McKeag, and Wm. Manson, aide to the lieutenant-governor.*

162 *Gordon Church of Lena, for many years a leading heavy horse exhibitor, drives His Excellency, Governor-General Roland Michener through the ribbon at the official opening ceremonies of the Keystone Centre.*

163 *The opening ceremonies, Keystone Centre, 2 April 1973. Present are, at the podium, National Defence Minister James Richardson, RCMP Superintendent Geo. W. Calbick, D.C. Lawson, Hon. Eugene Whelan, Hon. L.S. Evans, Mayor Bill Wilton, Mrs. W.J. McKeag, His Honor W.J. McKeag, Lieutenant-Governor of Manitoba, Governor-General Roland Michener, Mrs. Michener, Fred McGuinness, Master of ceremonies, James Moffatt, president, Provincial Exhibition of Manitoba, Wm. Manson, aide to the Lieutenant-Governor.*

THE TWO FAIRS HAD ALSO CHANGED, due in large measure to the impetus provided by the Keystone building project. In 1969, the two associations, the Provincial Exhibition of Manitoba and the Manitoba Winter Fair, merged operations as the Manitoba Exhibition Association. It was a logical, almost inevitable move, made more imperative by the financial and organizational demands of the move to the exhibition centre.

It was also a long time in the making. The two groups had worked closely together from the start, often sharing directors and having a common manager. The idea was not a new one, and had been discussed repeatedly in the past. Each time, however, a financial or personal consideration had interfered and the proposal was shelved. In 1969, the timing and need was right.

On 26 June 1969, George MacArthur asked the shareholders of the Provincial Exhibition to support:

> the amalgamation of the Provincial Exhibition and the Manitoba Winter Fair on the basis of combining the assets of the Manitoba Winter Fair and the Provincial Exhibition [and] that the new association be known as the Provincial Exhibition of Manitoba.

The Winter Fair board approved the idea in principle, setting the stage for more intense negotiations. Supporters of the proposed union hoped that a combined board would help marshall support for the Keystone Centre and would eliminate any further debate over the division between the two associations.

It would prove a difficult task. No merger would work until the different collective personalities of the winter and summer boards had been reconciled. The distinctions were important, and the organizational road-blocks substantial. The winter fair board consisted of delegates chosen by the numerous agricultural associations involved with the exhibition. The summer fair board, in contrast, was elected at a public meeting by shareholders in the Provincial Exhibition. Any person could become a shareholder and stand for office simply by purchasing a membership in the

164   *A.J. Poole, horse exhibitor, director, president of the winter fair, 1972.*

198

association. In practice, of course, it was quite difficult to garner enough support to win election to the exhibition's board of directors. There were other problems, the chief one being a rather striking imbalance in assets and cash. The summer fair had an impressive collection of buildings and ownership of its grounds, but the hard times of the previous decade had left it cash-poor. The winter fair, on the other hand, had a substantial bank account, but few physical assets.

Despite these obvious difficulties, there were compelling reasons why this merger should proceed. The pending loss of the Wheat City Arena, the enormity of the campaign to build the Keystone, and the obvious cooperation that would be required when the new facility was completed provided strong motivation to overcome the barriers. A further push was provided by several Brandon aldermen who were apprehensive that maintaining two separate organizations would mean a continuation of separate requests for financial aid from city hall.

Overriding all these political and administrative niceties, however, was the compelling argument that a consolidated board would do a much better job of serving the agriculture community. That position emerged particularly in the arguments and actions of Reginald Forbes. At the 1969 winter fair board meetings, Forbes accepted the presidency on one condition; he asked for, and received, permission to work toward "a marriage of the Manitoba Winter Fair and the Provincial Exhibition." As an agrologist and extension worker, Forbes was only too aware of the problems facing agriculture and as a long time exhibition supporter, knew the potential of fairs in overcoming some of those difficulties. In his position as principal of the Agricultural Extension Centre, he studied the current statistics and at the 1969 winter fair meeting shared his opinions with the audience:

When the winter fair started in 1908, 65 per cent of the population of Manitoba and 75 per cent of the population of southwestern

165 *Buddy Heaton and "Old Grunter," an attraction at the 1963 winter fair. On the final evening, a challenge race between "Old Grunter" and Jim MacArthur's quarter-horse, "McDooney", was held and "Old Grunter" came in second.*

199

Manitoba were farm people, and strictly farm-related practices at fairs made sense. Today, 17 per cent of the people of Manitoba and 23.5 per cent of the people of southwestern Manitoba live on the farm and to carry on the same show as formerly does not make much sense.

Despite the logic which suggested that changing times demanded changes to the fair, Forbes and his supporters faced some spirited opposition to the consolidation of the fair boards. When the winter fair board passed a motion favoring the merger, it squeaked through by a 12-11 margin. Spearheading the opposition was P. A. McPhail, a staunch traditionalist with impeccable exhibition credentials, who feared that the directors of the summer show were casting covetous eyes at the winter fair's cash reserves, a tidy $70,000.

The matter was settled by the "dreary science" of economics. The winter fair was losing money and losing its home. The summer fair owned nearly 90 acres of prime urban property which would soon provide the site for the Keystone Centre. Viewed in retrospect, the directors do not appear to have had as many options as they believed at the time. In either case, the majority of the winter fair board agreed with the need to move immediately. Lawyer Charles O. Meighen held meetings with representatives of the two boards, guiding them as they passed a series of bylaws which made possible this administrative marriage.

On 29 October 1969, the first meeting of the Manitoba Exhibition Association was held. The reconstituted Provincial Exhibition of Manitoba, now responsible for both the winter and summer fairs, came into existence. K.T. Macpherson was chosen to lead the new fifty-member board, which included all former members of the Provincial Exhibition of Manitoba and the Manitoba Winter Fair Association.

The mettle of the newly amalgamated board was soon tested. Though the construction of the Keystone Centre interfered somewhat with summer fair activities, the size of the grounds and the mildness of the season permitted considerable flexibility. The same was not true for the Winter Fair. The Wheat City Arena had been leveled almost immediately after the land was sold, but the Keystone Centre remained at least two years away from completion. Macpherson and company had to "make do" in makeshift quarters.

For 1970, the entire operation had to be relocated on the summer fair grounds. A secondary hockey arena called Man-Ex, with a seating capacity of only 1500, became home to the horse show. The smaller facility may have deterred some fair-goers from attending the popular shows, but the arena was filled to capacity during the main events. For stabling, the exhibition also had to make do with less than perfect conditions. The unheated and uninsulated barns built for the summer show were pressed into emergency service. Additional space was provided when a structure inelegantly known as the "old roller rink" was relocated from the old winter fair site to become an addition to the burgeoning Keystone complex.

Financing the full winter fair in inadequate facilities proved an onerous task, and one which taxed the capacity of the fair managers. The financial problems were eased somewhat by numerous signs of community support and encouragement. Letters to the editor before and after the show congratulated the directors on their fine effort, and a *Brandon Sun* editorial called on area residents:

> not to stay home just because things aren't as nice as they might be this year; you'll find the spirit and fun of the winter fair are just as big as ever in 1970.

The immediate difficulties also faded as the directors faced the reality that in short order they would have the magnificent Keystone complex at their disposal.

200

166 *A poster promoting the 1967 winter fair.*

167 *A feature attraction at each year's winter fair is the egg show. This picture shows the display at the 1967 show.*

168 *Opening ceremonies, winter fair, 1967. On the platform, Mrs. S.A. Magnacca, Hon. J.J.Greene, Minister of Agriculture for Canada, Mayor S.A. Magnacca, winter fair president Hope Turner, and Glen Milliken, soloist. In the landau: Mr. and Mrs. Ritchie Macpherson, Mr. and Mrs. Roy Clark, with Orville Fowler driving 'Miss Judy' and 'Electra Seaton Flicka'.*

169 *John Lehner, of Prince Albert, jumps his mount over a table at the 1967 winter fair. At the left end of the table is director James Moffatt.*

FINDING A NEW HOME proved to be only the first of the jewels added to the crown of Brandon's fairs. On 11 July 1970, a telegram reached the the directors of the Provincial Exhibition of Manitoba. It read in part:

> On the advice and recommendation of the government of Manitoba and the government of Canada, Her Majesty has graciously extended to the Manitoba Winter Fair the designation 'Royal.'

Henceforth, the Manitoba Winter Fair would be known as the Royal Manitoba Winter Fair. It was a stunning coup for the Brandon show, and a worthy distinction offered to an important western Canadian institution.

The royal designation came about as the result of a visit to Manitoba during its centennial year, 1970, of Queen Elizabeth. Several Provincial Exhibition directors learned that the Manitoba government was interested in seeking royal patronage for a praiseworthy institution. Because they believed that this high honor should go to a non-metropolitan recipient to off-set the earlier recognition of the Royal Winnipeg Ballet, the directors asked the exhibition to endorse an application on behalf of the winter fair. There was no hesitation.

The task of compiling an appropriate application fell to George MacArthur, the general manager, and two directors, F. McGuinness and D.C. Lawson. Together, they wrote a brief history of western Canada's oldest winter agricultural show. When it was delivered to Provincial Secretary Steinkopf, he added the endorsation of the province and dispatched it to Government House.

Formal acceptance was received a short time later. In a letter of congratulations, Canada's minister of agriculture, Hon. C.A. (Bud) Olson, said:

> …over the years the winter fair at Brandon has come to be known as one of the finest in Canada. It reflects, in my opinion, the efforts and cooperation of the citizens of all Manitoba in presenting a cross-section of prairie life, both rural and urban.

170 *Jimmy Moffatt takes evasive action during the next jump.*

Manitoba's minister of agriculture, Hon. Sam Uskiw, added his felicitations :

> I know that I share along with many Manitobans a pride of having the Manitoba Winter Fair elevated to royal status in this our centennial year. May I extend my best wishes to its continuing success as we are approaching Manitoba's second century.

On behalf of the board of directors and the administration, general manager George MacArthur said:

> This is one of the greatest things ever to happen any time, any place in western Canada.

The 1970s were off to a roaring start. With a new facility, and Royal patronage for the winter fair, Brandon's pair of exhibitions had a bright future. The winter fair, marked by a distinctive new logo which highlighted its royal status, simply took off. The Keystone complex reflected the time and care of D.C. Lawson's building committee, for it was well suited for exhibition purposes and agricultural competitions. The horse shows maintained their popularity, but the crowds increased thanks to the expanded capacity of the Keystone Arena.

The summer fair was slower in finding its feet. Ironically, the new Keystone complex provided tremendous competition for the summer event. A series of home, auto and sports shows stole attention away from the commercial displays at the exhibition, while the yearly round of concerts, circus, and other special events that could now be hosted in the new building detracted from the uniqueness of the mid-summer extravaganza. There was nothing malicious or out of place about this competition. The Keystone Centre, managed by a tri-partite board with representatives appointed by the province, the city and the Provincial Exhibition, had its own budget to balance, and could do so only if the buildings were kept busy throughout the year. It nonetheless added uncertainty to the ongoing efforts of the fair organizers to recapture that special niche long occupied by the summer show.

THE PROVINCIAL EXHIBITION OF MANITOBA also faced new demands and opportunities. By the early 1970s, there were noises emanating from one of the exhibition's major constituencies that changes were called for, and soon. The concerns came from the livestock exhibitors, long-time supporters of the Brandon fairs.

The issue first emerged formally in 1973, following the submission of a report by Donn Mitchell, chairman of the livestock committee. Mitchell commented, both with pleasure and concern, on the growing number of cattle entries for the summer fair. While pointing out that this would soon necessitate the construction of more stable space, Mitchell also reminded the exhibition shareholders that the so-called "exotic" breeds—Simmental, Maine Anjou, Chianina, Blonde d'Aquitaine and others—would need additional competitive classes. The combination of an increasing number of entries and an expanding number of breeds might, he commented, soon force the development of a livestock show separate from both the summer and winter fairs. The winter fair had held fall shows regularly over the years, primarily sheep, swine and cattle sales, but this new proposal suggested a larger annual event.

Mitchell's report proved timely, for it reminded directors of the growing number of complaints among livestock exhibitors. Only three months earlier, the board had dealt with a letter of complaint from several cattle exhibitors who protested that their cattle on show at the summer fair and been tied up too long for the amount of money involved.

This renewed talk of a fall fair—ironically the starting point for Brandon's exhibitions back in 1881—fit perfectly with a long held dream of P. Alex McPhail. A man with over half a century of association with the fairs as exhibitor, director, president and manager, McPhail had over many years promoted the idea of a return to the fall fair. His appeal was based in part on tradition, as he harkened back to the long-established season's-end fairs of Ontario and, he might have mentioned, Brandon before 1889, and the logic of timing. He argued that only when the fall grain

171　*Canada's largest egg show, proudly displayed at the 'Royal' Manitoba Winter Fair.*

172　*Dr. Gerald Dressler, president, Provincial Exhibition, 1974-75.*

ða 1985 23 March

When Hope Moffat was interviewed by a journalist prior to the winter fair, he told of the transportation routine he followed in earlier times to get his entries to the winter fair.

He used a team and sleigh to get his horses and cattle from the farm to the CPR depot at Carroll, where they were loaded into a box-car. The train took them to Souris where they were re-loaded on another train which took them to Brandon. On their arrival they were unloaded near 12th Street and Pacific Avenue and led through the city streets to the arena.

ða 1985 23 March

Birkett Mitchell has vivid memories of the 1943 winter fair; it took two men and a boy two days to deliver a calf from Brandon to Douglas.

Mr. Mitchell had been asked by his brother Ernie to help deliver the entry of Ernie's son, Don. They had to dig their way through a drift which blocked the roadway to Douglas; once there, they learned that the road to Brandon was plugged and they had to wait overnight for the plows to come through.

harvest was complete did livestock men have time to groom and show their cattle properly. McPhail's impassioned plea, backed by Mitchell's report and the protests from cattle producers, convinced the exhibition directors to investigate the matter.

Consultations were held with Frank Muirhead and Morris Deveson, senior representatives of the Manitoba Department of Agriculture. For obvious reasons, the idea had to clear the Manitoba Beef Growers Association. With solid support from both government and producers, the exhibition decided to proceed. On 13 February 1974, the directors voted to support "in principle" a new fall show to be held for the first time in 1975. Acceptance of the idea was far from universal. A small group of directors were apprehensive about the influence a fall show would have on other exhibition events. No one knew with confidence what effect the additional competition would have on entries to the summer and winter fairs, even though the Provincial Exhibition had been hosting small fall fairs for decades. They recommended caution. The opposition added a much needed cautionary note to the discussion, and forced the directors to examine slowly and carefully the finances and mechanics of the proposal.

By July 1974, some decisions had been reached. The fall show, to be called Ag-Ex, would have its own budget, but would be supported by exhibition financing if this were necessary. Discussions between livestock chairman Donn Mitchell and the federal government resulted in the ruling that a portion of the exhibition's livestock grant from the federal department of agriculture could be transferred to the new show. Members of the breed associations interested in supporting Ag-Ex travelled to Winnipeg to petition provincial politicians for support.

The Provincial Exhibition association had tapped just the right vein of sympathy and support. Producers, government and agri-business all saw the logic in a specifically agricultural fall show. On 3 November 1975, the first edition of the new show was

173   *Gordon Church, Lena, heavy horse exhibitor, president Provincial Exhibition 1975-77.*

174   *James Figol, electrical contractor, director Provincial Exhibition, president 1977-79.*

175   *Robert Flock, Douglas, president, Provincial Exhibition, 1980-81.*

officially opened. The entire Keystone complex was required for stabling, judging and sales. Auctions from five breeds of purebred cattle, hogs,market steers and carcasses drew a total of $307,824. The show lost money, as some of the detractors had predicted, but it had actually started off well. Ag-Ex quickly became a fixture on the Manitoba livestock scene. Commercial firms took note of the producers' obvious interest, and scrambled for space to exhibit their farm-related merchandise. The debates and discussion leading up to Ag-Ex had paid off, for the net result was a fall show which appealed directly to the audience it was designed to serve: the farmers and livestock breeders.

Ag-Ex was not the only example of the directors of the Provincial Exhibition of Manitoba knowing their audience and structuring their show accordingly. The success enjoyed by the winter fair through the 1970s and early 1980s demonstrated the same sensitivity to the desires of that feisty mixture of fair-goers from Brandon and surrounding districts. In a somewhat different fashion, the restructuring of the summer fair which brought that event back from the brink of collapse illustrated the difficulties and eventually success in keeping an age-old institution in step with the times.

176   *David Montgomery, president, Provincial Exhibition, 1982.*

As THE BRANDON FAIRS MOVE into their second century, a lot of familiar elements remain very much in evidence. The continuing attempts to combine the often very different interests of townsfolk and rural residents can be seen in each show. Such popular stand-bys as the Traveller's Day Parade, held for the 30th consecutive time in 1985, the ever-popular horse show of the winter fair, the innumerable entries in the cattle, poultry, hog, and horse competitions, the rides, games, noises and smells of the carnival, the echoing sounds of fairground musicians, the Kinsmen Club's car draw and the commercial exhibits remain in evidence.

177 *A large crowd gathers on the lawn on the south side of the Keystone Centre to watch the "Combine Crunch," a popular innovation at the exhibition.*

1985 23 March
George MacArthur recounted in a press interview the exploits of the famous jumping horse, Barrah Lad. In an exhibition of jumping one night in the Wheat City Arena, Barrah Lad jumped over a Buick car owned by Brandon's Mansoff family.

178   *"Amigo" entertains the evening horse show crowd.*

179   *A jumping demonstration at the winter fair.*

180   *Unusual action in the Keystone Arena, 1982.*

But there are abundant signs of change as well. The "hootchi-cootchi" girls are gone, victims of a more permissive age which no longer thrills to their titillations. So too are the horse races, and grandstand shows, the food booths run by the local churches, the Indian camp near the fairground and numerous other elements associated with the summer and winter exhibitions. But there are features in their place. A professional rodeo, the popular "King Farmer" competition sponsored by CKX radio and television, larger, faster and noisier rides and the "Combine Crunch" are but a few of the new events and attractions added to the program in the last few years.

The summer and winter fairs are important civic and regional institutions. For decades, Brandonites and western Manitobans have had the fair dates marked prominently on their calendars, and have considered the events a central part of their social and cultural life. To retain their popularity and their viability, the shows have had to change with the times, adapting to suit the demands of fair-goers, the needs of farmers and livestock breeders and the realities of an increasingly competitive entertainment marketplace.

The fairs therefore represent more than just the collected works of a group of enthusiastic and dedicated exhibition directors, more than the result of endless political wrangles and set-backs. To be successful, an exhibition must hit a nerve; it must satisfy the needs of the community in which it its set. The longevity of the summer and winter fair tells us that the exhibitions have had a solid, if not always completely comfortable home in Brandon; the success of recent ventures by the Provincial Exhibition of Manitoba suggests that the Provincial Exhibition, Royal Manitoba Winter Fair and Ag-Ex have carved their own niche in the life of western Manitoba and will continue to thrive so long as they remain sensitive to the needs of the community and the region.

Two historians of exhibitions in British Columbia once remarked:

The fair is in essence an image of its setting, providing a glimpse of how people view themselves and their region, what they feel they have accomplished and what they see as still to be done.

The Brandon fairs tell us a great deal about the city and surrounding district, about the influence of agriculture on the region's development, and the continuing attempt by the townspeople to satisfy their urban aspirations while remaining loyal to their rural roots.

Western Manitoba's fairs — the Provincial Exhibition of Manitoba, Royal Manitoba Winter Fair and Ag-Ex — have come a long way from their modest beginnings in 1882. The move from corner lot and borrowed warehouse space to the Keystone complex has been gradual, eventful and colorful. The development of the exhibitions mirrors the evolution of Brandon and area, charting the transformation of the region from a sparsely-inhabited prairie district to a major regional centre sitting amidst a vital agricultural district. The fairs have been an integral part of that change, encouraging improvements in farming and livestock, rewarding the best that the western plains has to offer, and responding to the urban ambitions of western Manitoba's largest city.

211

ello 1985 23 March
   *Miss Muriel Patmore,
between 1946 and 1973,
registered every agricultural
entry entered in either the
summer exhibition or the
winter fair. She later told a
reporter that, "Many of the
happy memories are of those
exhibitors...it was a pleasure
to work with them because
they were so appreciative."*

181 *The six-horse teams
line up at the 1966 winter
fair.*

The most common sources for illustrations are identified by abbreviations as follows—

Brandon University Archives: BrUnArc

Provincial Exhibitions of Manitoba
   Collection: PrExManC

Manitoba Archives: ManArc

Illustration
Number

1,2	Manitoba Archives
3-5	Brandon University Archives/ Provincial Exhibitions of Manitoba Collection
6-8	ManArc
9	BrUnArc/PrExManC
10,11	BrUnArc
12	H.R. Hoffman Ltd., Brandon
13	BrUnArc
14	BrUnArc/PrExManC
15	ManArc
16-19	BrUnArc/PrExManC
20	ManArc
21	BrUnArc/PrExManC
22-24	BrUnArc
25	BrUnArc/PrExManC
26	Daly House Museum, Brandon
27	BrUnArc/PrExManC
28	Assiniboine Historical Society
29-31	ManArc
32	BrUnArc/PrExManC
33	Daly House Museum, Brandon
34	BrUnArc/PrExManC
35	BrUnArc
36,37	BrUnArc/PrExManC
38	BrUnArc
39	unidentified
40	BrUnArc/PrExManC
41	The *Brandon Sun*
42	BrUnArc/PrExManC
43	The *Brandon Sun*
44	ManArc/Jessop Collection
45	BrUnArc
46	The *Brandon Sun*
47	BrUnArc/PrExManC
48	BrUnArc
49,50	ManArc
51	BrUnArc/PrExManC
52	BrUnArc
53-55	BrUnArc/PrExManC
56	BrUnArc
57	ManArc
58,59	BrUnArc/PrExManC
60	Collection: Mrs. Gwen McCallum McTavish
61	BrUnArc
62	BrUnArc/PrExManC
63	BrUnArc
64	The *Brandon Sun*
65,66	ManArc
67	BrUnArc/PrExManC
68	Dixon Collection
69-71	BrUnArc/PrExManC
72-73	BrUnArc
74	The *Brandon Sun*
75-77	BrUnArc/PrExManC
78	BrUnArc
79	BrUnArc/PrExManC
80	ManArc
81	BrUnArc
82,83	The *Brandon Sun*
84	BrUnArc/PrExManC
85	The *Brandon Sun*
86	BrUnArc/PrExManC
87,88	The *Brandon Sun*
89	BrUnArc
90-92	BrUnArc/PrExManC
93	BrUnArc
94-98	BrUnArc/PrExManC
99	BrUnArc
100	unidentified
101,102	BrUnArc
103	ManArc
104	BrUnArc
105-110	BrUnArc/PrExManC
111	BrUnArc
112	BrUnArc/PrExManC
113,114	BrUnArc
115,116	BrUnArc/PrExManC
117	ManArc
118	BrUnArc/PrExManC
119-121	BrUnArc
122,123	BrUnArc/PrExManC
124-128	BrUnArc
129,130	BrUnArc/PrExManC
131-133	BrUnArc
134	BrUnArc/PrExManC
135	BrUnArc
136	BrUnArc/PrExManC
137-140	BrUnArc
141	Collection: P.A. McPhail
142,143	BrUnArc
144	Collection: P.A. McPhail
145-147	BrUnArc
148	The *Brandon Sun*
149	BrUnArc/PrExManC
150,151	BrUnArc
152a	The *Brandon Sun*
152b-159	BrUnArc
160-163	BrUnArc/PrExManC
164,165	BrUnArc
166	BrUnArc/PrExManC
167	Collection: Jake Hiebert
168-171	BrUnArc/PrExManC
172-176	BrUnArc
177	Collection: Jake Hiebert
178-181	BrUnArc

215